INVESTMENT APPRAISAL

INVESTMENT APPRAISAL

A GUIDE FOR MANAGERS

Rob Dixon

Published by Kogan Page Ltd
in association with
the Chartered Institute of Management Accountants

|C| I |m|A|

Incorporated by Royal Charter
63 Portland Place
London W1N 4AB

To Bob and John

© Rob Dixon 1988

All rights reserved. No reproduction, copy or transmission of this publication may be made without written permission.

No paragraph of this publication may be reproduced, copied or transmitted save with written permission or in accordance with the provisions of the Copyright Act 1956 (as amended), or under the terms of any licence permitting limited copying issued by the Copyright Licensing Agency, 7 Ridgmount Street, London WC1E 7AE

Any person who does any unauthorised act in relation to this publication may be liable to criminal prosecution and civil claims for damages.

First published in 1988 by
Kogan Page Ltd, 120 Pentonville Road, London N1 9JN
in association with the
Chartered Institute of Management Accountants,
63 Portland Place, London W1N 4AB.

Printed and bound in Great Britain by
Biddles Ltd, Guildford, Surrey

British Library Cataloguing in Publication Data
Dixon, R.
    Investment appraisal: a guide for managers. 1st ed.
    1. Investment   2. Risk management
    I. Title
    332.6   HG4528
    ISBN 1-85091-468-01

Contents

Preface	*page* 9
1. An Introduction to Decision-making	11
Capital Markets	14
Capital Markets in Theory	15
Efficient Market Hypothesis	17
2. Traditional Approaches	20
Payback	20
Return on Investment (ROI) Method	23
Conclusions	25
3. Discounted Cash Flows	26
Time Value of Money	26
Net Present Value	28
Internal Rate of Return	30
Independent Projects in a Perfect Capital Market	33
'Unorthodox' Cash Flows	33
Single-period Capital Rationing	35
Differences in Scale of Investments: Mutually Exclusive Project with Different Cash Flow Patterns	36
Projects with Different Initial Capital Outlays	38
Unequal Lives	39
Dependent Projects	40
Summary of Merits of NPV	41
Summary of Merits of IRR	42
NPV *v* IRR	42
Conclusions	43
4. The Cost of Capital	45
Equity	47
The Cost of Each Type of Finance	48

The Weighted Average Cost of Capital	54
The Use of WACC in Investment Appraisal	56
Capital Structure in Theory	59

5. Decision-making in Conditions of Risk and Uncertainty — 64
Methods for Dealing with Uncertainty	65
Conclusion on the Game Theory Approaches to Uncertainty	70
Measures for Dealing with Risk	71
The Capital Asset Pricing Model	75
Risk	76
Sensitivity Analysis	79
Monte Carlo Simulation	81
Expected Values for NPV	82
Decision Tree Analysis	83

6. Capital Rationing — 88
Hard and Soft Rationing	88
Single-period Capital Rationing	89
Multi-period Capital Rationing	92
Linear Programming and Investment Strategy	93

7. Applications of Investment Appraisal — 98
Inflation	98
Taxation	103
Replacement Decisions	106
Lowest Common Multiple	107
Annual Equivalent Annuity	110
Lease or Buy Decisions	114

8. Investment Appraisal in the Public Sector — 117
The Stages in a Cost-benefit Study	120
The Choice of the Discount Rate	123
The Treatment of Distributional Effects	124
Conclusions	124
Examples	125

9. Control of the Investment Process — 127
Project Authorisation	128
Project Control and Post-audits	128
Post-audit Planning	130

10.	**Theory and Practice**	**132**
	Payback	133
	Accounting Rate of Return	133
	Discounting Methods	134
	Risk Appraisal Techniques	135
	Post-audits	136
	Conclusion	137
	Appendix	138
	Index	140

Preface

The text is an attempt to explain the techniques of investment appraisal in a simple and straightforward manner. Investment decisions are important to the future of organisations and to the expectations of investors. It is therefore crucial that managers should be knowledgeable about the techniques of investment appraisal and the consequences of their use. The main advances in theory are explained to enable readers to gain a broader insight into the processes of decision making in this key area of financial management.

I am extremely grateful to Peter Hall and Peter Rippingate for a great deal of work in the early stages of this manuscript and to Colin Drury for his helpful comments. My thanks also go to Mark Wright of CIMA for his support throughout this project. Any errors are, of course, my own.

1.
An Introduction to Decision-making

The need to make decisions is an ever-present part of business life. Some, though important, will be routine and mundane and can safely be delegated to the appropriate level. The most crucial business decisions relate to investment, for they determine the future of the firm. These decisions should be taken at the highest level. The purpose of investment is, in essence, to forego present consumption in order to increase the total amount of goods and services which can be consumed in the future. Investment is implicitly looked at from the point of view of the owners of the company. The shareholders (or sole owners or partners where there is no divorce between ownership and management) are prepared to forego present dividend payments and possibly share-price growth, and during the course of the investment to pay interest charges on money borrowed in order to finance capital projects, in the hope of receiving a significant return when these investments come to fruition. Investment will account for a major part of company funds and may well have a telling impact on future cash flows. Decisions, once made, may be irreversible, or at least costly to amend. Investment decisions may affect the structure of the company, its *raison d'être*, as well as, of course, its profits. Risk is also attached to every investment decision, though this will vary from the negligible risk of buying government stock to the plain foolhardy, which it is hoped will not be undertaken.

Sutcliffe and Bromwich in *Issues in Finance* (1986), edited by Firth and Keane, identify three aspects of investment. The first aspect is the creation or identification of a set of projects for deliberation; the second is deciding which, if any, of these projects should be undertaken; and the last is the organisation and implementation of the decisions taken. This volume will concentrate on the second of the three aspects. It should be noted here, however, that review of past decisions may be a

Investment appraisal

valuable part of the decision-making process, having important implications for current decisions. Questions can be meaningfully asked, such as – With hindsight, was the decision good? If it was not good, why not? Could any mistakes have been avoided? What can be done to avoid such mistakes in future? – and so on.

It can be seen, then, that making the correct decisions about investment will be crucial for the success of the business. Classical explanations of decision-making are based on four assumptions which basically add up to the decision-maker having perfect knowledge of all possible relevant information and acting appropriately in the light of this information. They are that the decision-maker has full knowledge of all the investment options open to him (ie he has not overlooked any options); that the consequences of those investment options are perfectly known and can be quantified in measurable terms; the results of the investment can be graded from the least to the most profitable; and that the decision-maker acts 'rationally'. Perfect and complete information enables the decision-maker to make the most profitable decisions for his business. Profit is assumed to be his primary goal, and he is said to be an optimiser – in other words, all his decisions and actions have the underlying objective of maximising profit. In practice, the decision-maker may be a satisficer rather than an optimiser; that is to say, he takes an easier, less problematic option which of course is also a less profitable one. His motto is 'anything for a quiet life'. As investment appraisal involves techniques that aid the decision-maker in identifying the most profitable investment, the habitual satisficer can be ignored in decision-making theory.

In the real world, the preceding assumptions about the completeness of information and knowledge concerning investment decisions are not wholly credible. The reasons for this are as follows:

1. Not all the outcomes of an investment decision can be assessed in profit and loss terms. An investment manager, for example, might feel, for non-financial reasons, that he would rather make his investment in a country whose political system he sympathises with than in one whose system he finds morally unacceptable. Some investments, then, may be viewed as intrinsically more valuable than others for

An introduction to decision-making

reasons which do not arise from the profit and loss account.

2. Knowledge concerning the possible investment options may by no means be complete. This could be due to a lack of market research, the presence of which might have highlighted a new market waiting to be developed; or the reason might be more prosaic, being the result of a lack of communication between departments or managerial grades within the business. Furthermore, the outcomes of an investment decision may not be certain. This could be for a variety of reasons, such as uncertainty about the strength of the economy, uncertainty about exchange rates if the investment relies on exports for sales (or imports for parts) etc.

3. The decision-maker may lack the mental capacity, or may be unaware of the decision-making techniques, needed to evaluate, rank and compare the various options which are open to him.

Investment appraisal techniques endeavour to overcome these limitations. There are a number of methods which attempt to allow for the effects of uncertainty on investment decisions. These techniques – sensitivity analysis, risk analysis, probability, and decision trees – will be discussed in detail later. Suffice it to say that the problems caused by uncertainty are not necessarily insoluble. The lack of practical know-how as to the evaluation of different investment options is remedied by the application of one or more of a number of investment appraisal techniques, namely, the payback method, the rate of return method, the net present value method and the discounted cash flow. Some methods are more sophisticated and meaningful than others. Their method, character, and strengths and weaknesses will be fully discussed later. As to the objection that some decision-making criteria are impossible to quantify, that is a matter for judgement after the financial merits and demerits have been estimated. The importance of non-financial aspects has to be considered, but must remain a matter of personal judgement and therefore outside the scope of this work.

The text will attempt to show how investment appraisal techniques can both simplify the complex problems of invest-

Investment appraisal

ment decisions and allow for the uncertainties of business life. This does not mean to say that theory should supplant judgement and the know-how that is born of experience; it does, however, form a logical basis for decision-making. It is unfortunate then that the widely available techniques, such as discounting, are so inadequately used. As long ago as 1965, the National Economic Development Council was reporting that,

> 'Many firms appear to apply criteria for assessing investment projects which have little relevance to the measurement of the expected rate of return to the capital invested.'

In 1982, Scapens, Sale and Tikkas, in *The Financial Control of Capital Investment* for the ICMA, surveyed 211 UK divisionalised companies. With average turnovers of £286 million and average capital expenditure per annum of £19.37 million, these companies were among the very largest in the British economy. Yet, of these high-powered companies, only 51.7% used discounted cash flow techniques (net present value and internal rate of return), while 55% used payback methods. Moreover, 24% of them used non-financial criteria for assessing investments. Even allowing for the survey's method of compilation which allowed multiple responses to questions, it is clear that among the top companies, the use of the more sophisticated investment appraisal techniques was deficient. Furthermore, it would seem reasonable to assume that as the size and scale of industry decreases, the use of investment appraisal techniques diminishes accordingly. Such techniques could profitably be used throughout industry.

Capital Markets

Businesses make investments with money that is raised from three sources. The first source is money generated by the businesses themselves through their commercial operations: retained profits. These are funds kept by the company after interest payments, tax payments and dividend payments have been taken from gross profits. The second source is additional capital invested by the owners of the business or new investors purchasing shares at an issue date. The third source of money is loans. These come from a variety of sources, collectively known

Capital markets in theory

as capital markets. Capital markets exist to transfer capital from those parties with surplus funds to those people or businesses who need extra funds to carry out their investment or expenditure plans. Without intermediaries, surplus funds would remain unused and idle, the equivalent of hoarding gold in a buried chest. The intermediaries make their profit essentially by lending at a higher rate of interest than that at which they borrowed.

This first section will look at capital markets from the point of view of modern financial theory, making use of economic models.

Capital Markets in Theory

The Perfect Capital Market

The theory of perfect capital markets is the starting point in understanding investment decisions and how they should be made. The perfect market is an economic model based on a set of assumptions, the object of which is to help explain how businesses make their decisions. The major assumptions are as follows:–

1. An individual can borrow or lend as much money as he wants at a common rate of interest which does not vary over time.

2. There are no transaction costs associated with raising finance for investment.

3. The market does not experience inflation or taxation.

The implication of this form of capital market is that any investment opportunity which is deemed to be profitable should be undertaken since the firm has access to as much capital as it requires. Figure 1.1 is a table which in a highly simplified way shows which investment options should be accepted and which should be rejected in a perfect capital market. The prevailing common interest rate is assumed to be 10%.

In a perfect capital market the rational investment manager will accept any investment which brings in a higher return than the market rate of interest. Thus, in the example below he would accept options A to E, making a total profit (after interest payments) of £251.50.

Investment appraisal

Project	Investment required	Amount to be borrowed	Interest rate	Amount to be repaid (capital interest)	Receipt from investment	Return on investment	Net profit after interest charges
	£	£	%	£	£	%	£
A	1000	1000	10	1100	1150	15	50
B	2500	2500	10	2750	2850	14	100
C	1800	1800	10	1980	2034	13	54
D	2000	2000	10	2200	2240	12	40
E	750	750	10	825	832.50	11	7.50
F	1500	1500	10	1650	1650	10	—
G	1750	1750	10	1925	1907.50	9	(17.50)
H	1250	1250	10	1375	1350	8	(25)

Figure 1. Investment options in a perfect capital market

In reality capital markets are not, of course, perfect. Nor could such markets ever exist in the real world. The chief objection to the perfect model is not that taxation and inflation do exist. These assumptions are made to simplify reality; they do not challenge the validity of the model, for the model could be redesigned to allow for these variables. It would merely make it more complex. The real objections are that interest rates are not available at a uniform rate, and that loans are not available in limitless amounts. It was in response to these objections that the imperfect capital market theory was formulated.

The Imperfect Capital Market Theory

This refines the capital market theory by stating that there is no single market rate of interest. Interest rates are likely to be available at a range of levels. In practice this will mean that the funds available to businesses for investment purposes will be limited. The corollary of this is that investment managers will have to be more discerning; that is, they will have to decide which investment opportunity is the most profitable over its whole life. Investment opportunities will have to be graded in terms of their desirability. The timing of cash flows as well as the total sum of cash returns will have to be considered. Thus, the imperfect capital market model is a starting point for the realisation that investment decisions are made on the consideration of a number of factors. The implications of the imperfect capital market model will be spelled out in some detail later.

Efficient Market Hypothesis

When the principles of perfect capital markets are applied to share prices on both the Stock Exchange and Unlisted Securities Market (USM), and to commodity prices, the resulting idea is the efficient market hypothesis. In essence this hypothesis is based on the assumption that participants in the market have perfect information concerning a firm, and that the market price of each firm's shares will immediately respond, in the appropriate direction and magnitude, to new information relating to the specific firm, the market sector in which it operates, or the overall economic climate. A market is said to be 'efficient' if share prices in that market fully and instantaneously reflect all information relevant to those shares. (NB It is important to realise that even if the market is not 'perfect' it can still be 'efficient'. There may be allocative imperfections whereby one firm is able to make monopolistic profits, but so long as share prices reflect this fact then the market can still be 'efficient'.)

The major implication of the efficient market hypothesis is that share prices are the best estimate of the underlying intrinsic value of those shares. Share prices represent the consensus view of the market as to the true value of the shares, given the information known about the firms concerned. If share prices do indeed reflect the intrinsic value of the shares then this fact should ensure that funds are invested in the most profitable securities, thereby resulting in an optimal allocation of limited economic resources.

A second important implication of the efficient market hypothesis is that present and future share prices do not depend upon past share prices. All currently available information will already be discounted into the prevailing share price. Consequently, share prices will only change in response to brand new information, which is just as likely to be adverse as favourable. The next share price adjustment is just as likely to be down as it is to be up, even if the share price has shown an upward trend over the preceding days, weeks or months. Therefore share prices are said to follow a 'random walk' pattern

Investment appraisal

– the direction of the next price movement cannot be predicted by analysing previous price movements.

Because share prices instantaneously reflect all relevant information and follow a random walk pattern, investors will not be able *on average* to make excess returns (ie returns over and above expected returns) by following a strategy of trying to 'pick winners' or by trying to identify undervalued shares. Of course an investor who adopts such a strategy may, by chance, make excess returns on some shares, but any such gains will be cancelled out by losses on other shares, leaving an average excess return of zero.

The efficient market hypothesis, which was originally formulated in an attempt to explain the random walk phenomenon, has been developed over the years, and three levels of market 'efficiency' have been identified:

1. Weak form efficiency;
2. Semi-strong form efficiency;
3. Strong form efficiency.

Weak form efficiency exists when current share prices fully reflect the informational content of past prices. Consequently, if a market is efficient at the weak form level, investors will be unable on average to make excess returns through analysing past share prices. Consequently, technical analysis and mechanical trading rules such as Chartism should not be used as a basis for buy/sell decisions.

A market is efficient at the semi-strong level if share prices fully and instantaneously reflect all information which is *publicly* available. This includes annual reports, press releases, stockbrokers' reports, announcements of mergers and acquisitions etc. Consequently, if a market is semi-strong efficient it is not worthwhile for the individual investor to undertake further fundamental analysis, since share prices already reflect all the information which is publicly available, so the search for undervalued shares will not be fruitful. Fundamental analysis is the evaluation of current and past data in connection with a company in order to predict future share prices.

A market is strong form efficient if share prices fully reflect all information. This includes 'inside' information which has not yet been made available to the public. If the market is efficient at the strong level, even 'insiders' such as directors could not profit by trading on the basis of inside information, as the implications of any new inside information will instantaneously be reflected in the share price.

There has been a great deal of academic research into the efficiency of capital markets. This research has tended to suggest that British and American stock markets are indeed efficient at both the weak and semi-strong level. They are, however, probably not efficient at the strong level, and it is possible to make profits through insider dealing (even though this practice is illegal). Consequently, share prices reflect all relevant publicly available information. Furthermore, the best indication of the intrinsic value of a share is its market price. As the information is available to all participants in the market, an investor will only be able to make an excess return by chance.

The implications of the efficient markets hypothesis (EMH) in so far as they affect investment appraisal are:

1. EMH in its strong form implies that there is no ideal time to go to the market for new equity, since future prices are just as likely to be above or below the current price. In its 'semi-strong' form if management is aware of favourable information which it has not made public then it might be better to wait until this information is released before going to the market for new funds.

   Resources should not be used to try and locate the most profitable shares. There is no point in looking to acquire under-valued companies unless synergy applies. Instead, a balanced and diversified portfolio should be put together. This should then be left well alone, thereby minimising trading costs.

2. If securities were not fairly priced, we could no longer use the return available in the financial market as a benchmark for setting the discount rate, or rely on the share price to increase once the market is aware that the firm has undertaken profitable projects.

2.
Traditional Approaches

Investment was defined in Chapter 1 as the sacrificing of consumption now to allow a greater amount of consumption in the future – making an outlay of cash in the expectation of extra cash coming in. Investment appraisal techniques naturally try to estimate whether the cash returns from the investment will be large enough to make the initial investment worthwhile. They serve as a guide to decision-making; they should not be regarded as inviolable or as techniques set down from on high.

Two very popular and easy-to-use techniques are the payback method and the return on investment method (or accounting rate of return). They do not make use of complex theory or mathematics, and therein probably lies their appeal. Though they are by no means without faults, their continued popularity is assured.

Payback

Payback simply measures the number of years it is expected to take for the original costs of investment to be recovered. It has two main uses. First, it can be used as a basis for accepting or rejecting a single investment. The investment manager might decide that an investment with a payback of five years was unacceptably long and reject the proposal. Payback policy might be laid out by the directors of the firm and applied to all decisions. In this case, the investment manager has an easy task. He has merely to reject all proposals which take longer than the time decreed to be acceptable. The trouble comes if one makes the reasonable assumption that certain investments will have a longer payback period than others by their very nature. A new factory which necessitates construction, the recruitment and training of employees, the purchase of sophisticated plant and machinery etc will have a longer payback period than will the

Payback

addition of one extra machine into that factory at a future date. Secondly, payback can be used to rank projects and help decide which, if any, of a number of options should be accepted.

As an example, let us consider Dilston Ltd which has two investment options. Each requires an investment of £20,000. The net cash inflows from projects A and B are estimated to be as follows:

Year	A £	B £
1	6,000	2,000
2	7,000	3,000
3	4,000	5,000
4	4,000	6,000
5	1,000	6,000
6		5,000
7		5,000

Project A would take three and three-quarter years to recoup the original investment. Project B would take four and two-thirds years. If the firm employed a four-year payback, project A would be accepted and project B rejected. The first disadvantage of payback is evident from the example. Any time limit for payback is bound to be arbitrary. In the case of Dilston Ltd it led to the rejection of the more profitable project B which would have shown an income of £32,000 in seven years. Project A would have made only £22,000 in five years. Thus project B showed a clear £10,000 more profit than project A. Projects which take a number of years to make a return are characteristically those which involve the development of new products or markets, and these are likely to be the very decisions vital for future success. Unfortunately the payback method ignores all cash flows which arise after the payback period. It is sometimes referred to as a 'fishbait' method because it is primarily concerned with recovering the 'bait' rather than with the size of the 'fish' that might be caught!

A second, and no less important, weakness of the payback method is that it takes no account of the time value of money. This concept will be explored in detail in the next chapter; suffice it to say that £1 is valued more highly now than in, say, one year's time. This is because £1 invested today at a 10% rate

Investment appraisal

of interest would be worth £1.10 in one year's time. Were you to be offered £1 now or £1.10 in a year's time, you would have no preference. £1 now would be said to be worth £1.10 in one year from now. Thus, the timing of the cash inflows is important as well as the absolute amount of these inflows. To illustrate this, let us take two investment options. Each cost £1,000. The cash inflows are as follows:

Year	A £	B £
1	750	350
2	150	350
3	100	300
4	100	100

The payback method ranks these investments equally since they both have exactly the same payback period. Project A is, however, obviously more attractive. It has faster cash inflows: 68% of the value of the investment is recovered in the first year with option A as opposed to 32% with option B. In year one the company will have a clear £400 extra to do with as it pleases. The time value of money dictates that option A is by far the best choice.

A further disadvantage of the payback method of appraisal is that it is not consistent with the concept of profit maximisation. If the directors of Paul Tones Audio Ltd specify a required payback period of five years or less on investment projects then they would reject a project which offered an annual return of 15% (and therefore had a payback period of six and two-thirds years) even if they could raise the required capital at a cost of only 10% per annum.

Payback will continue to be used, for it is easy both to apply and to understand. Its use can be justified as a rule-of-thumb method of appraisal for the more minor, everyday investment decisions which confront a firm. To use more sophisticated techniques might be a waste of time and effort, unjustified by the smaller sums involved.

Payback has one important benefit in that it helps to allow for risk and uncertainty, albeit in an unsystematic way. It may make sense to try and recover the initial outlay as soon as possible if the investment is taking place in a politically and/or economically unstable country, or if the investment is in a market where rapid

Return on investment (ROI) method

technological advances quickly make state-of-the-art products obsolete. (On the other hand, it could be argued that projects which have a short payback period may be relatively risky. A short payback requires a high rate of return on investment, and high rates of return are often associated with a relatively high degree of risk.)

Return on Investment (ROI) Method

This method has a number of other titles which it might be useful to know for recognition purposes. The accounting rate of return has been mentioned; the return on capital expenditure (ROCE) has not. It also has a number of possible methods of calculation. It is an average rate of return calculated by expressing average profit as a percentage of average capital employed in the investment. Profit is generally defined as profit after depreciation charges but before taxation and, of course, dividends. Any increases in working capital necessitated by accepting the project are included in the capital employed. It should be noted that when calculating the average capital employed, any scrap value of the investment should be added to the cost of the investment. This is because depreciation will not be charged for the residual value.

To take an example, Gatling Ltd wish to buy a new machine for shaping wood. The investment costs £20,000 and is expected to last five years, being scrapped at the end of its life. Depreciation is charged on a straight-line basis (that is, equal amounts of £4,000 are charged in depreciation for each of the five years of its life). The profits after depreciation charges are set out on the next page.

The ROI method can be used as a decision-making tool by setting a minimum ROI. In the example, if the minimum was 15%, then the wood-shaping machine would be purchased (since ROI exceeds the minimum acceptable level). It can also be used to grade different investment proposals. The proposal with the highest ROI would be accepted where projects were mutually exclusive or where only a limited amount of capital was available for investment.

This system is frequently used because, like the payback method, it is easy both to apply and to understand. Another advantage is that management are often assessed on the overall

Investment appraisal

Year	Profit £
1	1,250
2	1,500
3	2,000
4	3,000
5	2,500

Total profit = £10,250

Average capital employed = $\dfrac{20,000}{2}$ = £10,000

Average annual profit = $\dfrac{10,250}{5}$ = £2,050

Return on investment = $\dfrac{\text{estimated average profit}}{\text{estimated average investment}} \times 100$

ROI = $\dfrac{2,050}{10,250} \times 100$ = 20.5%

return on capital employed by the company, and it thus makes a great deal of sense to make investment decisions on the same grounds. An advantage it has over payback is that it measures cash inflows over the whole life of the investment (not just the period up to the point of payback), and does not arbitrarily reject an investment which is more profitable in its last years of life than in its first. The payback and ROI methods are often used together, the intention being that the strengths of each combined will help iron out their individual flaws and provide a better basis for decision-making.

The return on investment method is, needless to say, not without disadvantages.

1. There is no authoritative method of calculating capital employed or of defining profit.

2. It does not take into account the time value of money.

3. It does not differentiate between large and small investment decisions, the flow of profits or the length of life of the

investment. For example, the ROI approach would rank a 15% return on £100 for five years higher than a 14% return on £10,000 for 20 years.

Conclusions

Although payback and ROI provide uncomplicated information useful in decision-making, there are too many significant flaws associated with them for their use to be wholly satisfactory. They do not take into account all the factors which are relevant when making investment decisions. Unless their deficiencies are fully recognised, they may mislead managers into making decisions which are far from optimal. What is needed then is a technique which takes into account the timing of all cash flows which result from investment decisions.

3.
Discounted Cash Flows

Time Value of Money

We saw in the last chapter that money has a time value. That is, £1 is valued more highly today than at a time in the future, but lower than at a time in the past. A number of reasons for this can be identified:

1. Money can be profitably invested between now and the future and will give a return at a given rate of interest. If one had the choice of being given £100 now or £100 in a year's time, the present interest rate being 10%, one would take the £100 now and invest it so that it would become £110 in a year – ten pounds more than one would get by taking the second option. Therefore the present value of £110 receivable in one year is £100 when the interest rate is 10%.

2. Individuals and firms naturally prefer money, with which they can consume goods, now rather than at some time in the future. If someone needs money for a bus fare now, it is little consolation for him to know that he will be able to afford the fare next month.

3. Inflation is an ever-present factor in modern economies. Inflation of course erodes purchasing power. An inflation rate of 5% means that £1.05 will be needed in one year's time in order to purchase the same quantity of goods and services that can currently be purchased with £1.

4. The world is uncertain. It is important for a firm to have £1,000 now rather than in one year from now. There is always a certain risk that the unthinkable might happen and the firm become bankrupt, or some other misfortune befall it.

This principle is used by businesses so that they can compare all

Time value of money

future cash flows on a common basis; that is, give all future (or past) sums of money a present value. This is of supreme importance when assessing the profitability of investment projects whose lives last a number of years.

Future, and past, values of money expressed in present values are found by using the concept of compound interest. If £1 is invested at 10% per annum and is left to accumulate interest, the following table can be drawn up to show how the principal grows:

Future value of £1 at compound interst of 10%

Year	
0	1.00
1	1.10
2	1.21
3	1.33
4	1.46
5	1.61

[handwritten: $\frac{10}{100} \times 110 = 0.11$ Then add on 11p to £1.10 = £1.21]

This principle is known as compounding. What we have said is that if we know that we can get a return of 10% on an investment, then five years on £1 held now will be worth £1.61. Thus, compounding measures the future value of money invested at some point in the past.

The future value of a sum of money invested at a certain rate of interest (or being said to have a time value of x%) can be found from the formula:

$$FV = V(1+i)^n$$

where
  FV = future value
  V = sum invested
  i = interest rate
  n = number of years of the investment

The reverse side of this principle is known as discounting. This gives the present value of money receivable at a future point in time. The present value of £1 receivable in one year when interest rates are at 10% is 91p.

The following table shows the present value (the value today)

Investment appraisal

of £1 receivable at various points in the future at an interest rate of 10%:

Year when £1 will be received	
0	1.00
1	.91
2	.83
3	.75
4	.68
5	.62

This can be derived from the formula:

$$PV = \frac{FV}{(1+i)^n}$$

To take the example of the present value of £1 receivable in five years time at a market rate of interest of 10%,

$$PV = \frac{1}{(1+0.10)^5} = 0.6209 \text{ or } 62p$$

Compounding and discounting are related mathematically, one being the reciprocal of the other for the same year. Thus, in year five,

$$\frac{1}{0.62} = 1.61 \text{ and } \frac{1}{1.61} = 0.62$$

Instead of using formulae to work out present values of money, tables have been drawn up which show compounded and discounted money values at various rates of interest. They appear as an appendix at the back of the book.

The two principal methods of discounted cash flow are net present value (NPV) and internal rate of return. That is, they are investment appraisal techniques which take into account the concept of the time value of money.

Net Present Value

The net present value (NPV) of a project can be defined as 'the value today of the surplus that the firm makes, over and above what it could make by investing at its marginal rate'. The firm's

Net present value

marginal rate is the lowest acceptable rate of return on investment; this will usually be its opportunity cost of capital (the cost of rejecting the next most profitable investment) because, according to the profit maximisation theory, the firm should continue to use an input until its marginal cost equals its marginal revenue. Cost of capital can be defined as the weighted average of the costs of all the sources of capital which the firm uses. This includes shareholder's equity, retained profit, debentures, fixed interest loans, and overdrafts etc. The method of assessing this will be shown in Chapter 4. The NPV method involves forecasting all future net cash flows of the project under consideration, ie revenues minus all costs, including the investments required. NPV make use of cash flows rather than accounting profits, so there is no need to deduct sums for items not involving the movement of funds, such as depreciation. The cash flows are then discounted to their present value using the firm's cost of capital as the discount factor. The formula for calculating NPV is:

$$NPV = \frac{A}{1+r} + \frac{A}{(1+r)^2} + \frac{A}{(1+r)^3} + \ldots + \frac{A}{(1+r)^n} - I$$

This may be summarised as:

$$NPV = \sum_{t=1}^{t=n} \frac{A_t}{(1+r)^t} - I$$

where

A_t = the net cash flow in year A
t = time (in years)
n = the point in time when the project comes to the end of its life
r = the firm's marginal rate of discount (annual rate of discount)
I = the initial cost of the investment

The NPV method gives a definite decision rule. All projects

Investment appraisal

with a positive NPV should be undertaken as these projects will increase the shareholders' wealth as this reflects the present value of future cash flows.

To take an example, Rip Ltd operates in a market where products have a short economic life due to changing public tastes. The firm has sufficient spare productive capacity to undertake an investment which has been proposed by one of the directors. The only cost of the investment is an initial cash outflow of £75,000 which will be required to promote and advertise the new product. This investment will produce net cash inflows of £10,000 in year one and £55,000 in each of years two and three. The cost of capital for Rip Ltd is 20% per annum.

Therefore the NPV of the proposed project is calculated as follows:

Since the NPV of the project is positive, it should be accepted as it will result in an increase in the shareholders' wealth.

Internal Rate of Return

A second method making use of discounted cash flows is the internal rate of return (IRR). It can be defined as the rate of return that is being earned on capital tied up, while it is tied up, after allowing for the recoupment of the initial investment. IRR is the value of r in the NPV equation which results in a NPV of zero – ie it is the discount rate which discounts all future net cash flows into equality with the initial capital investment. The IRR, then, is an attempt to find the discounted rate of return on the investment. It does not, essentially, produce new information compared with the NPV. As Lumby in *Investment Appraisal* (1984) states, 'it may be questioned whether it is truly a method of appraisal at all or just an arithmetical result'.

Determining the IRR of a project is largely a matter of trial and error. The IRR is found by identifying the value of r so that

$$\sum_{t=1}^{t=n} \frac{A_t}{(1+r)^t} - I = 0$$

Internal rate of retu.

For example, the directors of Eros plc are trying to identify the IRR of a project with the following cash-flow profile:

Year	Cash flow (£)
0	(90,000)
1	50,000
2	40,000
3	30,000

By trial and error the directors find that a discount factor of 15% results in an NPV of £3,449 and a discount factor of 20% results in an NPV of −£3,144. This trial and error process is repeated until the directors arrive at a discount rate of 17.52% which gives an NPV of −£3 – close enough to zero to be treated as the IRR.

A slightly less accurate but much more expedient method of identifying the IRR of a project is based on the technique of interpolation. First, two discount rates must be identified, one of which results in a slightly positive NPV and the other which gives a slightly negative NPV. Clearly the IRR must lie somewhere between these two discount rates. If we make the assumption that the relationshp between NPV and discount rate is linear between these values (as shown in Figure 3.1). then we can use interpolation to calculate the IRR.

In the case of Eros plc a discount rate of 15% gave an NPV of £3,449. When the discount rate was increased by 5% to 20% the NPV fell to −£3,194 – a total decrease of £6,643.

The directors of the company wish to find the increase in discount rate (above 15%) which reduces NPV by £3,449, ie to zero. A 5% increase caused a total decrease in NPV of £6,643, so if the assumption of linearity holds true then the increase needed to reduce NPV to zero must be;

$$\frac{3,449}{6,643} \times 5\%$$

$$= 0.519 \times 5\%$$

$$= 2.60\%$$

Therefore the interpolation method would suggest an IRR of 17.60%. This result is in fact inaccurate by approximately 0.8%

Investment appraisal

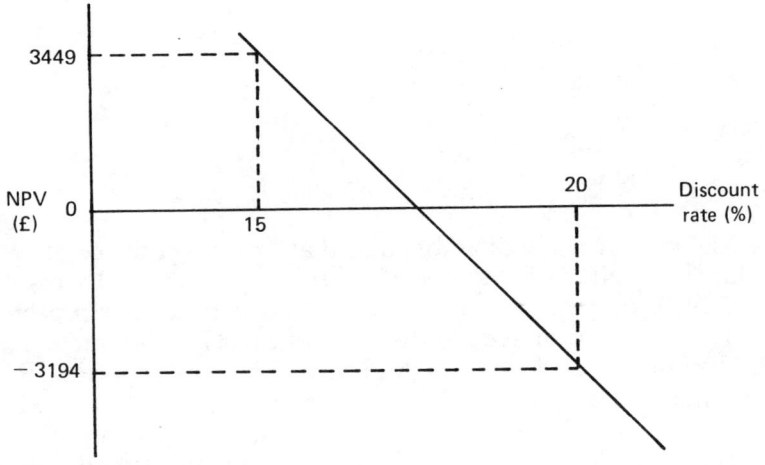

Figure 3.1 Net present value: discount rate (linear approximation)

(the actual IRR is 17.52%) but it is perhaps close enough to be acceptable. The inaccuracy arises out of the fact that the relationship beween NPV and discount rate is not actually linear but is as shown in Figure 3.2.

The error can be reduced by interpolating between two discount rates which give only very small positive and negative NPVs. However, for most purposes the inaccuracy of the estimate of IRR will be insignificant especially when it is remembered that forecasts of cash flows arising from the project will themselves be subject to some degree of error because of the existence of uncertainty.

Once the IRR of a project has been calculated it can be compared with the firm's cost of capital, and if the IRR is greater than the cost of capital the project should be accepted. Hence, the IRR method also gives a definite decision rule. Having defined and described the two 'scientific' methods of discounting, we can examine the effectiveness of each of them in order to identify which, if either, is superior.

'Unorthodox' cash flows

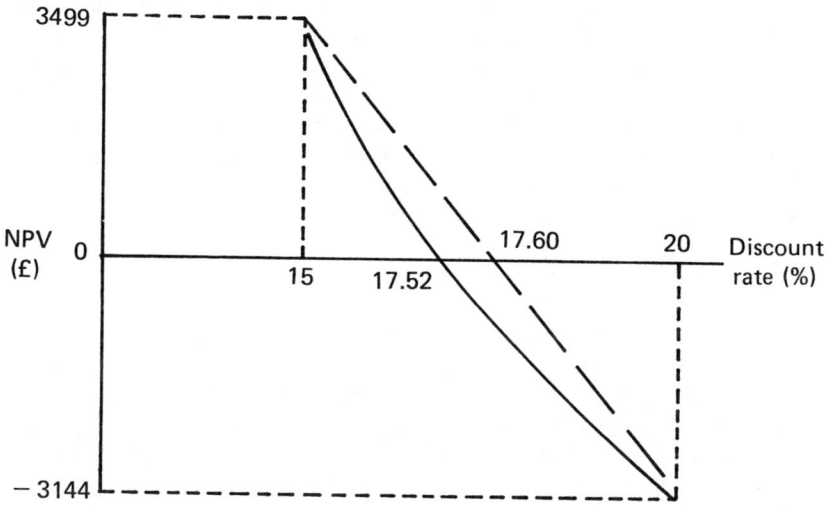

Figure 3.2 Net present value: discount rate

Independent Projects in a Perfect Capital Market

If all projects under consideration are independent of one another and funds can be raised to finance *any* profitable investment (as is the case in a perfect capital market) then both the NPV and IRR methods of appraisal are equally acceptable – any project with a positive NPV or an IRR which exceeds the cost of capital should be accepted, as this will increase the value of the firm. In this situation neither project has an advantage over the other.

'Unorthodox' Cash Flows

In certain situations the IRR method cannot be used to rank projects because there is no single unique IRR value which will give a NPV of zero. This occurs when the cash flows do not follow the conventional pattern of an initial cash outflow, followed by subsequent cash inflows – ie an 'unorthodox' cash flow occurs when there are additional net cash outflows in later years in the project's life.

The IRR of a project is actually the root of a polynomial

33

Investment appraisal

equation, and the number of roots, or solutions, depends upon the number of turning points that the equation has – this is known as Descarte's rule. A turning point occurs each time the cash flows change from positive to negative, and vice versa. Hence if the sign of the cash flows changes more than once there will be more than one IRR. As a general rule, there will be as many IRRs as there are changes in sign of cash flow. An example of such a cash flow is given below:

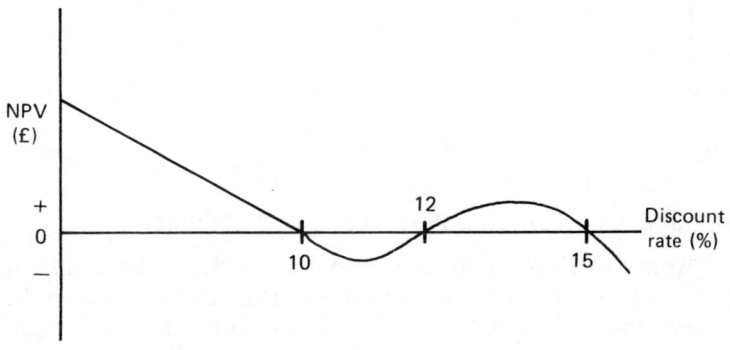

Figure 3.3 DFC with multiple IRRs

It is debatable which, if any, of these three values of IRR is economically meaningful.

Similarly, there may be a single IRR for a project but at no rate of discount does the project yield a positive NPV. In the case below, if the cost of capital was 10% the IRR method would accept the project since the IRR of 20% exceeds the cost of capital. However, the NPV method would correctly reject the project whatever discount factor was used, since at no point does the project have a positive NPV.

In practice, the variation between NPV at the various rates given as IRRs is usually small and the NPV is close to zero; consequently the problem is not too serious.

Single-period capital rationing

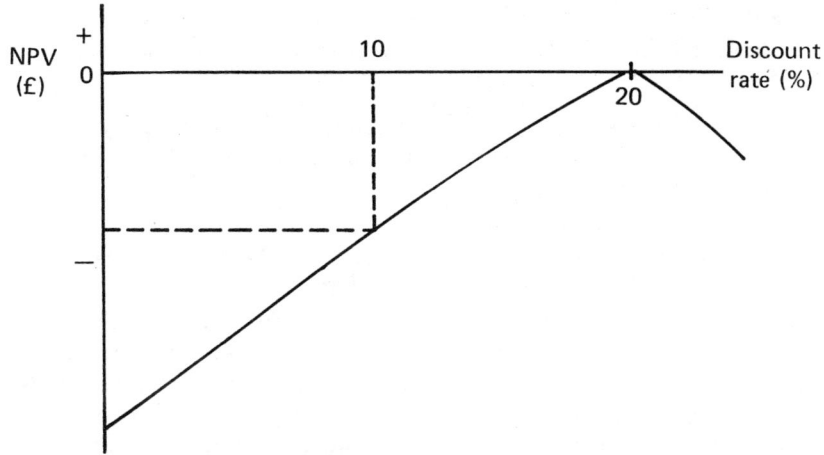

Figure 3.4 DFC with negative NPV

Single-period Capital Rationing

Under single-period capital rationing, neither appraisal method in its simple form will select the optimum project. For example, consider the case where only £100 is available for investment, and the following three investment opportunities are available:

Project A – investment of £100 with NPV of £20
Project B – investment of £50 with NPV of £10
Project C – investment of £50 with NPV of £15

The NPV technique in its simple form would select project A since it has the highest NPV and its capital requirement does not exceed the £100 which is available. However, we could achieve a higher total NPV if we were to select projects B and C instead of A. Total investment still only equals £100 but total NPV now equals £25 (ie £10 from B plus £15 from C).

The NPV method can easily be adapted to cope with this problem by calculating the NPV per £1 of investment for each project, and then selecting projects in descending order of this value until all available capital is exhausted. Hence in this case:

35

Investment appraisal

Project A has NPV per £1 of investment of £0.20
Project B has NPV per £1 of investment of £0.20
Project C has NPV per £1 of investment of £0.30

Therefore project C would be selected first, followed by B and then, since all the available capital has been exhausted, A would be rejected.

Differences in Scale of Investments: Mutually Exclusive Projects With Different Cash-flow Patterns

In many cases acceptance of one project automatically excludes acceptance of another, eg an oil company may have to decide whether to build a pipeline from its oilwell to its refinery or to buy a tanker to move the oil – it can only accept one of these alternatives. In a case such as this the IRR and NPV methods will not necessarily give the same ranking to the projects. This is best shown by an example:

Year	0	1	2	3	NPV (at 10%)	IRR (%)
	£	£	£	£	£	
Project A	−9514	+1000	+5000	+9000	2284	20
Project B	−9514	+7000	+5000	+1000	1730	23

In this case the IRR method ranks B above A, but the NPV method ranks A above B – ie the two methods give conflicting signals.

The NPV of these projects at every discount rate can be shown graphically – see Figure 3.5.

At a discount of 15.47% the NPV of the two projects is exactly equal. This rate has become known as the 'Fisher' rate. For discount rates below the Fisher rate project A has a higher NPV, but for discount rates above the Fisher rate project B has the higher NPV. Hence the IRR and NPV methods will give the same ranking only if the discount rate which is chosen exceeds the Fisher rate. At lower discount rates the two methods will give conflicting rankings. In order to overcome this problem we must consider the *incremental* cash flows of the two projects, ie the difference between the two cash flows:

Differences in scale of investments

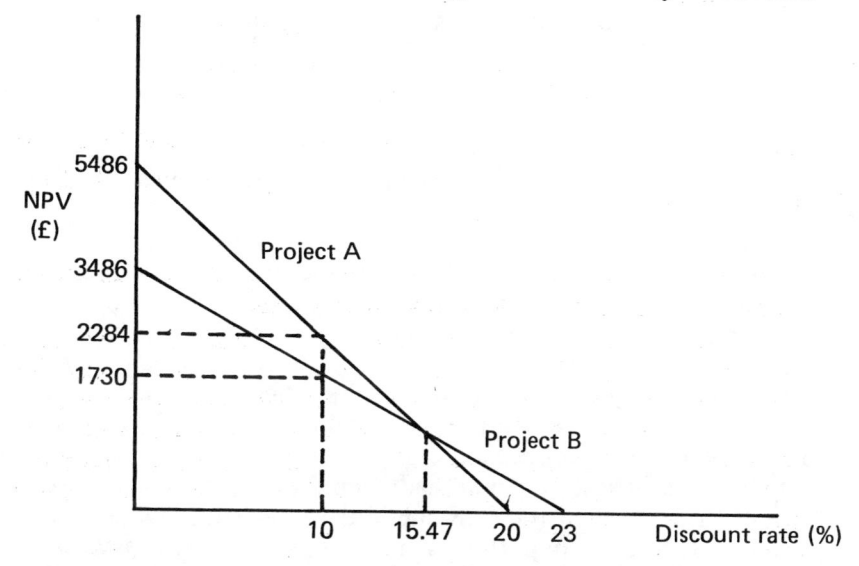

Figure 3.5 DFC for mutually exclusive projects

Year	0	1	2	3
	£	£	£	£
Project A	−9514	+1000	+5000	+9000
Project B	−9514	+7000	+5000	+1000
Incremental Cash flow (A−B)	—	−6000	—	+8000

Hence accepting project A would have the same result in cash-flow terms as accepting project B but reinvesting £6000 of the £7000 cash flow in year 1 in return for an additional cash flow of £8000 in year 3. We can think of this as a separate hypothetical project called (A–B). Therefore,

Project A = project B *plus* project (A–B)

We should compute the IRR of an £8000 return in two years' time on an investment of £6000 in order to decide whether this hypothetical project (A–B) is worthwhile.

Investment appraisal

Using the formula $6000 = 8000/(1+r)^2$, where r is the IRR of (A–B),

r = 15.47%

and since the firm's cost of capital is only 10%, project (A–B) is worth undertaking.

Therefore, if we applied the IRR rule we would initially accept project B over project A and we would then go on to accept project (A–B) as well. This is the same thing (in cash-flow terms) as accepting project A in the first place, which is the selection that the NPV method advocated in its basic form. Hence we have used the IRR method to prove that when there is a conflict of this sort between the IRR and the NPV techniques, the NPV method indicates the correct decision.

If the firm's cost of capital had been greater than 15.47% (but less than 23%) then the IRR method would still have accepted project B, but the hypothetical project (A–B) would have been rejected. However, from the graph we can see that the NPV method also ranks project B as being superior to project A at costs of capital in excess of 15.47%.

Therefore the NPV method *always* gives the correct decision, whereas the IRR method in its simple form will only give the correct decision if the cost of capital is greater than the Fisher rate. If the IRR method is to be used where there are many mutually exclusive projects, then the IRRs of *pairs* of projects and their incremental cash-flows must be calculated, and choices made between each possible pair of projects until the project which is better than all the others is identified. This can be an unacceptably long process if there are many different projects under consideration, as many different pair combinations must be compared. There seems to be little point in such an exercise since the NPV method will indicate the optimum project straightaway.

Hence, in the situation of mutually exclusive projects the NPV method is superior to the IRR method.

Projects With Diffrent Initial Capital Outlays

The problem caused by different scales of investment can be clearly demonstrated by the fact that the IRR method would

Unequal lives

select project X with a return of 20% on £100 over project Z with a return of 19% on £1000. It does so because it is a *relative* method which takes account of the 'quality' but not the 'quantity' of the investment, whereas the NPV method is an *absolute* measure, which takes account of the *scale* of the investment. Most investors would prefer the smaller return on the larger initial outlay, but the IRR method takes no account of the size of the investment. The only way the IRR could be legitimately used would be to compare project Z with project X *plus* an investment of £900 in the next best available project – only then would we be comparing two investments of £1000, and the IRR of project Z could be compared with that of the combined investment of project X plus the other £900 investment.

Unequal Lives

If we imagine two projects with unequal lives:

Year	0 £	1 £	2 £	3 £	4 £	NPV (at 10%) £	IRR (%)
A	−100	+120	—	—	—	9	20
B	−100	—	—	—	+174	19	15

we can see that once again the IRR and NPV methods contradict each other in their indication of the optimal investment. As previously, this is due to the fact that we have not taken account of the scale of the investment. IRR would select A because it has an IRR of 20% as opposed to only 15% for B. However, B gives a return of 15% for four years, whereas A gives a return of 20% for only one year. Hence the NPV of B is larger than that of A. The IRR has yet again ignored the scale of the investment because it gives a relative rather than absolute measure. NB The argument that A is better because it releases capital sooner, which can then be reinvested in other projects, is invalid in this case because in a perfect capital market additional funds could be raised to undertake these other projects even if B was selected (assuming that these other projects are not dependent upon the selection of

Investment appraisal

A). This fact highlights one of the common misconceptions about the *reinvestment assumptions* made by these appraisal techniques. Simon Keane points out that it is often stated that the IRR method implicitly assumes that the cash flows are reinvested at the IRR of the project, and that the NPV method implicitly assumes that they are reinvested at the cost of capital. This assumption is incorrect – neither method makes *any* assumption about the reinvestment of the cash flows arising from the projects which are undertaken. Reinvestments are subject to a separate decision at the appropriate time.

Dependent Projects

Should it be the case that a subsequent project (or projects) can only be entered upon if another earlier project has been undertaken, then these subsequent projects *must* be included in the cash flow predictions when deciding whether or not to accept the first project. It is erroneous to compare only the cash flow of the original projects which were under consideration – the cash flows resulting from all the subsequent dependent projects must also be included. For example, if we have to choose between projects A and X, but projects B and C can only be undertaken if A is undertaken, and project Y can only be undertaken if X is undertaken, then it is incorrect to reach our decision by only comparing A with X. We *must* compare A, B and C as one choice with X and Y as the other choice. Provided this is done the NPV method will *always* indicate the optimal decision (but as we have seen, the IRR method will not necessarily do so).

A similar situation arises when we have multi-period capital rationing. In selecting projects for immediate investment we have to take all future investment opportunities into account. In this case neither the NPV nor the IRR method is necessarily capable of giving the right investment choice. For example, we may feel it would be better to undertake a project with both a low NPV and low IRR if this would repay all the capital in a very short space of time thereby releasing it for investment opportunities in the near future. Of course, if we were very confident that these future opportunities would actually arise, we could include them in the cash flows used to select projects, in the same way as we do with dependent projects.

It has been demonstrated that the conflict between IRR and NPV arises because of:

1. different cash flow patterns
2. unequal initial outlays
3. unequal project lives.

In fact, these cases are all examples of the *scale effect*. The scale of a project refers not only to the size of the initial outlay, but also to the pattern of the cash flows and the duration of the project. In other words, the scale of a project depends upon the average amount of capital invested and the length of time for which it is invested. Two projects may have the same initial outlay, but if one of them provides large cash inflows in the early years this is in effect a repayment of capital, thus reducing the scale of the investment. If the initial cash flows are smaller then a large proportion of the initial capital remains invested for longer, and therefore the investment is of a larger scale. This consideration alone shows that the IRR method is invalid as a means of deciding between two investment opportunities because IRR is a *ratio* and the investment decision needs an *absolute* measure if the value of the firm (and therefore the shareholders' wealth) is to be maximised.

Summary of Merits of NPV

1. Clear, simple and unambiguous in meaning, quantitative values being given.

2. Consistency with the widely accepted business aim of profit maximisation as it involves maximisation of present values of future cash flows.

3. The discount rate used reflects the returns required by the suppliers of funds, ie interest rate.

4. The method incorporates time value of money and is thus superior to non-discounting methods but, in addition, technical difficulties of IRR are avoided.

Investment appraisal

5. Leads to optimal decision-making in that the present value of a firm's cash resources will be equal to (or larger than) the present values of the cash resources resulting from the use of any other method.

Summary of Merits of IRR

1. The discount rate appears as a percentage figure, it can be argued that percentage values are more easily understood, being readily comparable and less specific than quantitative values.

2. It can be argued that businessmen are more familiar with and used to the expression of rates of return, and unfamiliar with concepts of net present values.

3. Useful indicator of what margin of error there is in an investment decision, bearing in mind that all estimates are uncertain. The IRR is by definition the break-even discount rate on a project, the highest discount rate at which the project would be worthwhile. It therefore indicates the margin of error in estimates of the discount rate – it does not however indicate how sensitive or viable a project is to errors of estimates of cash flows.

4. Managers do not need to choose a discount rate to express the opportunity cost of capital and this reduces the subjectivity of the appraisal. (In NPV there is a decision to be reached on the appropriate opportunity cost of capital.)

NPV *v* IRR

In many circumstances the two appraisal techniques give the same advice but in some cases there is a conflict – these situations arise when choices between investment projects have to be made. In cases such as these IRR appears to have several limitations, NPV proving to be the better indicator.

The IRR method is a *relative* one, ie returns are measured relative to the initial investment outlay. The problem with this approach is that no account is taken of the magnitude of the initial outlay. Thus no distinction is made between large

Conclusions

investments with a good rate of return and small investments with a very good rate of return – this is a major disadvantage as businesses may prefer either the former or the latter and the IRR gives no consideration of that preference.

The IRR will give the same advice as the NPV whenever the latter is a smoothly declining function of the discount, ie the NPV decreases as the discount rate increases. However, not all cash flows have this characteristic since when *borrowing* (as opposed to lending as in investing) occurs the system is reversed. For example,

Project	C £	C1 £	IRR (%)	NPV at 10% £
A	−1000	+1500	50	+364
B	+1000	−1500	50	−364

Each project has an IRR of 50% but this does not mean they are equally attractive. In project A money is being lent while in project B money is being borrowed. When we are lending we want a high rate of interest but when borrowing we want a low rate. Plotting cash flows for project B on a discount rate/NPV graph shows that when *borrowing* the NPV increases as the discount rate increases, ie NPV is an increasing function as the discount rate increases.

In this case the IRR rule does not hold out because we want an IRR below the opportunity cost of capital and not, as before, an IRR above the opportunity cost of capital. Thus in this case the NPV appraisal method is more appropriate. Further problems arise with IRR when there are unorthodox cash flows, ie where there are multiple IRRs.

Conclusions

In all the cases which have been considered above the NPV has proved to be a better method of investment appraisal than IRR, as it always indicates the optimal investment alternative. The fact that the IRR method is a relative measure (as opposed to the absolute measure given by NPV) means that it cannot be used in its simple form when considering investments of different scales.

Investment appraisal

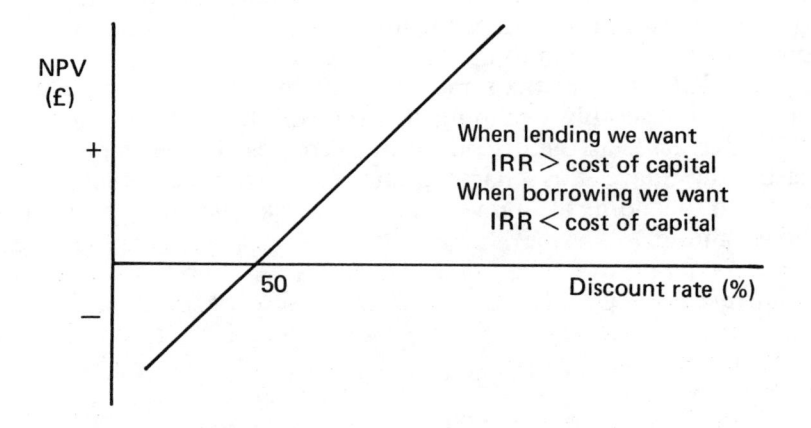

Figure 3.6 DFC for borrowing

Since nearly all investments *will* have either differing initial outlays, cash flows and/or lives, they will nearly always be of different scales. The IRR method can usually be adapted to take account of this, but these modified versions of the technique are often extremely 'unwieldy' to use, and there is little benefit in using them in preference to the straightforward NPV technique. The fact that the IRR method is used much more in practice than NPV indicates not that it is more widely understood, but that its flaws are not recognised, as in nearly all cases the NPV is theoretically as good as, or better than, IRR. If the IRR technique *was* fully understood then it is unlikely that it would be used to the extent that it is presently.

4.
The Cost of Capital

The previous chapter described and explained investment appraisal methods based on discounted cash flows. In order to calculate NPV and IRR it is necessary to know what a firm's cost of capital is since this is used as the discount factor. Firms obtain their funds by borrowing from two basic sources: they can either borrow from intermediaries (banks, venture capital providers etc), or they can borrow funds from shareholders, that is, the owners of the firm.

In almost all situations firms finance their investments from both sources. The mixture of these two elements is known as capital structure. The ratio of borrowed funds to either total funds or shareholders' capital is termed the 'gearing' ratio. A firm is 'highly geared' when it has a large proportion of funds borrowed from intermediaries in relation to its share capital. Alternatively, 'low gearing' occurs when the great bulk of borrowed funds is in the form of share capital.

In basic terms, the advantages and disadvantages of different levels of capital gearing are as follows:

1. The higher the level of capital gearing, the greater the risk associated with the company. At this stage it is important to differentiate between two types of risk – business risk and financial risk. Business risk is the inherent uncertainty surrounding the level of pre-tax profits which will be generated by the business. It arises because it is usually impossible to forecast accurately levels of demand for the firm's products, cost of inputs etc. Financial risk is the additional risk that is introduced as a result of the use of gearing in the capital structure. Therefore, while investment decisions determine the basic business risk of the firm, the level of fixed interest finance in the capital structure determines the financial risk.

Investment appraisal

Financial risk can be best illustrated using an example: Ging Ltd and Smith plc both operate in the same industry and therefore both face very similar degrees of business risk. The two firms are in fact identical in all respects other than the degrees of gearing used in their respective capital structures. Ging Ltd has no debt whereas Smith plc has as part of its capital structure £500,000 of 8% debt. Both companies have annual earnings of £100,000. The fixed interest financial charges incurred by each company are: Ging Ltd – nil; Smith plc – 8% of £500,000 = £40,000. Therefore Ging Ltd will make a profit after financing charges of £100,000, whereas Smith plc will only make £60,000. If earnings for both firms fell to 25% of their existing level, Ging Ltd would still show a profit of £25,000 whereas Smith plc would be unable to cover its debt charges.

Clearly the probability of cash insolvency increases with the level of gearing used by the firm, as does the variability of the earnings available for ordinary shareholders. Fixed interest loans have to be paid whether or not a profit is made but the company can avoid paying a dividend to providers of share capital in poor years.

2. When profits are being made, high gearing will provide shareholders with a high return on capital employed. This is mainly because interest payments on loans are deducted from profits before they are assessed for corporation tax. Thus, with corporation tax at around 50%, the cost of borrowing capital (ie the interest rate) is, to all intents and purposes, halved.

3. The presence of inflation erodes the cost, in 'real' terms, of borrowing. If a firm borrows money from a bank at an interest rate of 10%, and inflation is running at over 10%, then the firm is in effect borrowing funds free of charge.

For example, if a firm borrows £10,000 repayable in one year with an interest charge of 10% per annum it will repay to the lender £11,000 on maturity. However, if during that year inflation has been running at 12% then the real purchasing power of £11,000 in beginning of the year prices is only:

$$\frac{£11,000}{1.12} = £9,821$$

Therefore the lender has actually experienced a loss in purchasing power by lending to the firm. The borrower on the other hand has benefited because he is repaying less in 'real' terms than he borrowed. In practice the rate of inflation will not normally exceed the interest rate but even if it is less it still reduces the effective cost of borrowed funds.

Equity

Individuals buy shares in a company with two motives. First, they hope that the market-value price of the share will rise once they have bought it so that they will be able to sell at a profit at some time in the future. Secondly, they hope that the firm will be profitable, and that some proportion of those profits will be transferred to the shareholders in the form of dividends.

Once the company has issued shares it can further increase its equity by retaining some proportion of the profits it manages to generate (ie not paying them out as dividends) and/or by issuing more new equity.

When a new issue of shares is made, they can either by sold direct to the public, or existing shareholders may be given a prior right to buy the new shares. They may, for example, be offered one share for each five already held. New issues are sometimes viewed with suspicion by shareholders and potential purchasers because they may lead to a fall in share prices. If a new share issue is to be successful in overall terms it must leave the share price roughly at its former level, and preferably increase share prices and thus shareholder wealth. (Shareholders will, however, often be prepared to accept a short-term fall in the market value of their shares if they feel that the money raised through a rights issue will be used profitably to increase their wealth in the longer term.)

Retained earnings are by far the most important element in the expansion and growth of a firm. They cannot be said to have a direct cost to the firm itself, but they can be said to have an opportunity cost to the shareholders. The alternative to retaining profits is of course to pay dividends to the owners. If profits are retained they must (from the shareholders' point of view) be used

Investment appraisal

to bring in a greater return than the shareholder himself could gain by investing elsewhere outside the business at a similar level of risk. The return the shareholder will be looking for will be in the form of higher future dividends and a growth in the value of his shares.

The Cost of Each Type of Finance

In order to determine the overall cost of capital for a firm we must first identify the cost of each individual type of finance in the overall capital structure.

The Cost of Equity

The cost of equity is basically the return that shareholders expect the company to earn on their money. The method of assessing that cost, then, is based upon the market price of the share, the dividend payable on the share and how much the dividend is expected to grow in the future. This is known as the dividend growth model, or Gordon's model.

The formula for finding the company's cost of equity is,

$$K_e = \frac{Do\,(1+g)}{Po} + g$$

where

K_e is the company's cost of equity (ie shareholders' marginal rate of time preference);
Po (ex dividend) is the current market price of the company's shares;
Do is the current dividend;
g is the expected annual growth in dividend payments.

The first calculation to be made, before finding the cost of equity, is to find the expected annual growth in dividend payments. This is found by averaging the percentage increase in payments over a number of years. The assumption of constant growth is unrealistic and the model can be adapted to incorporate variable growth.

The calculation of the cost of equity can be shown using an example. Gower Ltd has 10,000 shares in issue at a current

The cost of each type of finance

market price of £2.50. Over the last five years total annual dividend payments have risen from £90,000 to £145,000.

The average growth rate may be calculated thus: dividend in year $1 \times (1+g)^4$ = dividend in year 5,

$$(1+g)^4 = \frac{\text{Dividend in Year 5}}{\text{Dividend in Year 1}}$$

$$= \frac{145,000}{90,000}$$

$$= 1.611$$

therefore

$1+g = \sqrt[4]{(1.611)}$
$1+g = 1.126$
$ = 0.126$ say 12.6%

The historic dividend growth rate is 12.6% and is assumed to continue indefinitely.

We now have enough information to calculate the cost of equity.

$$Ke = \frac{Do\,(1+g)}{Po} + g$$

$$= \frac{0.14500\,(1.126)}{2.50} + 0.126$$

$$= 0.191 \text{ or } 19\%$$

The cost of equity is 19%

Unfortunately, theoretical criticisms of this method of assessing the cost of capital have been expressed. These are all based upon the notion that past performance is no indication of future performance. Uncertainty about the future means that future dividends can never be predicted with any sort of accuracy or confidence. The further into the future one looks, the less sure one is of how dividends will perform. Despite this fundamental criticism, the dividend growth model does provide useful information about the cost of equity for investment purposes. There is another way of establishing the cost of equity capital

Investment appraisal

which takes account of systematic risk. This is known as the capital asset pricing model and is dealt with in Chapter 5: Decision Making in Conditions of Risk and Uncertainty.

The Cost of Preference Shares

From a cost of capital point of view preference shares are exactly the same as irredeemable debentures. Therefore their cost is given by the following formula:

$$Kp = \frac{c}{Po}$$

where

Kp = the cost of preference share capital;
c = the coupon rate on preference shares (ie the dividend rate);
Po = the current market price.

For the reasoning behind this formula refer to the explanation of the cost of debt capital.

The Cost of Debt Capital

Firms can generally borrow from external sources in two ways. Firstly, they can take out a loan at a given rate of interest to last for a given number of years. Secondly, they can issue debentures which commit them to paying interest to debenture holders for a number of years. Debentures may or may not be redeemable. For ordinary loans, the pre-tax cost of debt is the interest rate the firm has to pay. The cost of calculating the cost of debentures is more complicated.

Debenture holders receive a series of payments from the issuing company. This may be constituted by either a continuing stream of interest payments into perpetuity if the debt capital is irredeemable, or a finite stream of interest payments plus redemption of the face value of the debt repayable on the maturity date for a redeemable debt. The debenture holder makes an investment represented by the market value, the debenture, in order to receive these payments. The market value of a debenture therefore represents the present value of the

The cost of each type of finance

stream of cash flows that is to be received by the holder. The discount rate which discounts the cash flow stream into equality with the market value of the debt is the cost of issued debt capital. Therefore, by knowing the payments that are to be received by the debenture holders and the market value of the debenture, we can calculate the cost of capital which makes the current market price and the discounted future cash receipts equal. This model can be used to calculate the cost of both redeemable and irredeemable debentures, and preference shares.

The cost of irredeemable debentures is found using the following formula:

$$K_d = \frac{i}{Do}$$

where

K_d = the cost of debt capital
i = interest paid
Do = the market price of debt capital after payment of the current interest.

To take an example, if Elmsall Ltd have issued 8% debentures which have a market price of £96 cum interest, ie the price of the debenture includes the right to an interest payment, the cost of debt will be:

$$= \frac{8}{96.8}$$
$$= 0.0909 \text{ or } 9.1\%$$

When debentures are redeemable, there is no constant flow in perpetuity. If the Elmsall debentures of 8% with a market value of £96 were redeemable in five years time at £100, then the market value (£96) will be equal to discounted present value of future receipts (£8 a year for five years followed by the repayment of £100).

So, we must identify the interest rate which will discount the following cash flows,

Years 1–5	£8
Year 5	£100

51

Investment appraisal

into equality with the current market value of £96. In other words the discount factor is required which gives an NPV of zero for the following cash flows:

Year	£
0	(96)
1–5	8
5	100

This can be done using the method of interpolation described in Chapter 3. We shall first try discount rates of 5% and 10%.

Year	Cash flow	PV with 5% discount rate	PV with 10% discount rate
	£	£	£
0	(96)	(96)	(96)
1–5	8	34.636	30.326
5	100	78.353	62.09
		16.99	−3.58

These figures are derived from the formula described in the last chapter:

$$\frac{(96)}{1.00} + \frac{8}{1.10} + \frac{8}{(1.10)^2} + \frac{8}{(1.10)^3} + \frac{8}{(1.10)^4} + \frac{8}{(1.10)^5} + \frac{100}{(1.10)^5} = (3.58)$$

Clearly the appropriate discount rate (ie the IRR) lies somewhere between 5% and 10%, so we can use the process of interpolation to pinpoint this value. A 5% increase in the discount factor reduced the NPV from 16.99 to −3.58, a total decrease of 20.57. In order to reduce the NPV by only 16.99 we need to increase the discount factor by X% where:

$$X = \left(\frac{16.99}{(16.99+3.58)}\right) \times (10-5)$$

$$= 4.1\%$$

The cost of each type of finance

therefore the IRR = 5%+4.1% = 9.1%.

Thus the cost of redeemable debentures for Elmsall Ltd is 9.1%.

The Effect of Taxation on Debt Capital

Interest payments made to providers of loan capital such as short- and long-term loans, overdrafts, debentures etc, are deductable against tax. (NB dividends paid to ordinary and preference shareholders are *not* tax deductable.) This has a significant influence on their effective cost. For example, Grazummers Ltd has issued £1 million 8% debentures which have a current market value of £94 each. The company therefore incurs interest payments of £80,000 each year. However, it can deduct these payments from its taxable profit. If the prevailing corporation tax rate is, say, 40% this deduction will have the effect of reducing the company's tax liability for the year by £32,000 (40% of £80,000). Thus the effective cost of the debenture capital is not £80,000 but £48,000.

The effect of taxation can be reflected in the formula for cost of debt capital,

$$K_d = \frac{i}{D_o}(1-t)$$

where

K_d = the cost of debt capital (allowing for tax effect)
i = interest paid
D_o = market price of debt capital after payment of the current interest
t = applicable taxation rate.

Thus the cost of debenture capital for Grazummers Ltd (assuming that almost a full year's interest has accrued to the debenture holders) would be:

$$\frac{8}{94-8} \times (1-0.4)$$
$$= 0.056 \text{ or } 5.6\%$$

As a general rule debt capital will usually represent the cheapest

Investment appraisal

form of finance for the company followed in order of increasing cost by preference shares and ordinary shares. This is because the company undertakes to pay providers of debt capital a fixed rate of interest, and will often provide them with security for loans. Lenders also have a prior right to repayment of their capital if the company goes into liquidation. Therefore they carry a relatively small proportion of the risk associated with the company, and consequently they are not in a position to demand as high a return as other providers of capital who assume a great level of risk. A second factor which reduces the effective cost of fixed interest debt capital is that interest payments are tax deductable. Preference shareholders receive a fixed payment also, but they carry a greater level of risk than providers of loan capital, (a) because they may only be entitled to a dividend if dividends are declared, and (b) because they will usually only be entitled to repayment of capital on liquidation after secured lenders have been repaid. Therefore preference shareholders usually demand a greater return on their capital than providers of debt finance. Ordinary shareholders carry the greatest share of the risk (this is why ordinary share capital is often referred to as 'risk' capital). The directors of the company may decide not to declare a dividend if results are poor, and the ordinary shareholders rank behind both providers of debt capital and preference shareholders in terms of entitlement to repayment upon liquidation. Consequently, in return for carrying the bulk of the risk the ordinary shareholders will expect a greater return on their investment, making equity capital one of the most expensive forms of long-term finance for the company.

The Weighted Average Cost of Capital

Once the cost of each individual source of capital has been established, it is then possible to calculate the firm's weighted average cost of capital (WACC). A weighted average must be used in order to reflect the relative importance of each source of capital in the overall financial structure. If a simple unweighted averaging process were to be applied, then no account would be taken of the relative proportions of each type of capital used, thereby giving disproportionate importance to less significant sources of capital and understating the influence of those sources accounting for larger proportions of the total capital supply.

The weighted average cost of capital

After identifying the various types of finance used, the next step is to find the current market value of each of these sources of capital. Market value should not be confused with book value. The proportion of the total market value of the capital employed accounted for by each individual source of capital should be calculated in percentage terms. It is these percentages which enable us to weight each individual source of capital. Within decision making it is necessary to estimate the likely future WACC and the consequent need to use future weights within the calculation. The best estimate of future market values, and, consequently proportions within the overall capital structure, is current market values. The next step is to assess the impact of taxation on the sources of capital. The effects of taxation will be referred to here, but will be more fully discussed in Chapter 7. The weighted average cost of capital is finally found by multiplying the cost of each source of funds by its weighting factor and adding up the resulting figures.

To illustrate the calculation of the weighted average cost of capital, let us take as an example, S & F Ltd. It has ordinary shares with a market value of £3,000,000, 9% debenture stock with a market value of £200,000, long-term loans of £500,000 at 8% interest and a £300,000 overdraft at an interest rate of 11%. The rate of corporation tax is 50% and the assumed cost of equity after tax is 12%. From this information, a table can be drawn up which gives all the relevant details.

	Market value £000	(A) Weighting %	(B) Cost after tax %	(C) Weighted cost (A×B) %
Equity	3,000	75	12	9
Debentures	200	5	4.5	0.225
Long-term loan	500	12.5	4	0.5
Overdraft	300	7.5	5.5	0.41
	4,000	100		10.13

The weighting factor is found in the case of equity by

$$\frac{3,000,000}{4,000,000} \times 100\%$$

Investment appraisal

Corporation tax at 50% has the effect of halving the overall cost to the company of loan capital. This is because corporation tax is assessed on profits which remain after interest payments have been deducted. Multiplying the cost after tax by the weighting factor gives us the weighted cost of each source of finance. These weighted costs can then be added together to determine the weighted average cost of capital. In the example, the weighted average cost of capital is 10.13% for S & F Ltd.

(NB When market values are used retained earnings are *not* included separately in the WACC calculation since the market price of ordinary shares reflects the fact that ordinary shareholders own the retained earnings. Thus the value of retained earnings is, in effect, implicitly included in the market value of ordinary shares.)

The Use of WACC in Investment Appraisal

Although theoretical criticisms of the WACC concept have been voiced, it is an extremely useful tool in investment appraisal. It allows the investment decision and the financing decision to be separated for all but the largest projects. In using WACC as the discount factor in appraising investment projects it is implicitly assumed that the investor has a 'pool' of capital which consists of several different types of finance from various sources. When a project is undertaken the necessary finance is drawn from this pool, so in effect, the investment is funded by an average mix of all the various types of capital used by the company. Naturally the pool of finance will require regular 'topping up' in order to replace amounts drawn out for investment, but the decision as to the specific source (or sources) of finance which will be used to replenish the pool is quite separate from the investment decision. So long as the acceptance of a specific investment project will not cause a radical change in the capital 'mix' in the pool then the WACC can be used in appraising the investment. In practice this makes it suitable for investment opportunities which have the same risk characteristics as the average risk of the firm's existing assets. (The capital mix will of course change slowly over time so the WACC should be periodically re-calculated.)

Investments which are undertaken must earn a rate of return in excess of the company's WACC if they are to increase the

The use of WACC in investment appraisal

value of the firm for its owners. If, using the discount rate indicated, an investment shows a positive NPV, then the investment is worthwhile, for cash returns exceed those necessary to repay the suppliers of capital.

To illustrate the use of WACC in investment appraisal the following simple example is given. The management of Skinny Co Ltd are contemplating an investment in a new machine. It is estimated that the cash flows will be as follows:

Year	Cash flow (£)
0	(75,000)
1	12,000
2	20,000
3	40,000
4	30,000
5	10,000

In order to calculate the NPV of this project the management wish to determine the weighted average cost of capital for Skinny Co Ltd. The company's capital structure is as below:

	Market value
Share capital: 1 million ordinary shares of £1 each, fully paid	£1.80 each (ex dividend)
100,000 6% preference shares of 50p each fully paid	£0.46 each (ex dividend)
Debentures: £500,000 8% debentures issued	£97 per £100 nominal

Long-term bank loan: £250,000 – interest 13% per annum

The company distributes all its profits which have remained at a fairly constant level over recent years. The current dividend rate is 30%. Corporation tax of 50% applies. It is five months since the last interest payment was made to debenture holders.

Investment appraisal

Cost of Equity:

$$Kp = \frac{Do(1+g)}{Po} + g$$

$$= \frac{0.3(1+0)}{1.80} + 0$$

$$= 0.167 \text{ pr } 16.7\%$$

Market value of equity: 1 million shares at £1.80 each
= £1.8 million

Cost of Preference Shares:

$$Kp = \frac{C}{Po}$$

$$= \frac{0.06}{0.46}$$

$$= 0.130 \text{ or } 13.0\%$$

Market value of Preference Shares: 100,000 at £0.46 each
= £46,000

Cost of Debentures:

It is necessary to calculate the market value of the debenture after removing the increase in value due to the fact that five months' interest has accrued to the debenture holders.

'Stripped' market value = £97 − $(\frac{5}{12} \times 8)$

= £93.67

$$Kp = \frac{i}{Do}(1-t)$$

$$= \frac{8}{93.67}(1-0.5)$$

$$= 0.043 \text{ or } 4.3\%$$

Market Value of Debentures: 500,000 at £93.67 per £100
= £468,350

Cost of Bank Loan:

13% × (1 − 0.5) = 7.5%
'Market value' = £250,000

Like most decision-support systems, sensitivity analysis has certain drawbacks which must be borne in mind when using the technique. The major disadvantage is that sensitivity analysis in its simple form only allows for a change in one variable at a time while all other variables are held constant. Thus there is an implicit assumption that all variables are independent of each other. In reality this is not the case. For example, if sales price is increased we would also expect sales volume to decrease in response. Clearly it is important that interdependency between certain variables is always recognised when using this approach. A further qualification to its use is that sensitivity analysis provides no definite rule to guide the decision-maker as to whether the accept/reject decision should be altered in the light of its findings.

Monte Carlo Simulation

This is a form of simulation which uses computers to establish a probability distribution for each variable thought to be relevant. A random value from each distribution is selected by the computer which converts the values chosen into a series of cash flows which are used to calculate the NPV for that combination of outcomes. This process is then repeated until a probability distribution of the required decision criterion is built up.

As will be appreciated, this form of analysis is extremely complex. The number of simulations necessary to construct a clear picture is huge, and so the need for a computer with the necessary program, which should be readily available, is clear.

The benefit of Monte Carlo simulation is that it allows management to find the sensitivity of the results to the input factors by running the program with changes in their distributions. Further research can then be begun as and when critical variables are established. The information provided by Monte Carlo simulation is only as good as the initial estimates of the probability distributions which have been assigned to the individual input variables. It is not the case that figures are arbitrarily chosen, fed into the computer, and an error-free analysis of risk emerges. The technique, in other words, is only as good as the individual who operates it.

Investment appraisal
Expected Values for NPV

In the real world, management will not simply give a single estimate of how successful, or otherwise, an investment is going to be, and base all their plans upon this one estimate. Rather, they will put up a range of estimates. The project in question may depend for its success on the macro-economic state of the world. Let us take as an example Spetses Ltd which invests £5,000 in a project which has a three-year life. The following table will show estimates of the annual net cash flows based on three economic states of the world: boom, neutral conditions and recession. The NPV is calculated for each state and a probability of this state occurring is attached. These NPVs are then combined to give an average NPV (via an arithmetic mean). This is the expected NPV, or ENPV, from which point the usual decision to accept or reject can be taken as usual. Management's task is both to estimate the cash flows of the project and assign a probability factor to each state of the world occurring.

Year	0	1	2	3
Economic boom	(5,000)	3,500	2,500	2,000
Neutral state	(5,000)	3,000	2,200	1,500
World recession	(5,000)	2,500	1,500	1,250

using a discount rate of 15%, the following NPVs emerge:

Boom	£1,249
Neutral	£ 258
Recession	£ (870)

State of the world	*Probablility of occurrence*
Boom	0.25
Neutral	0.50
Recession	0.25
	1.00

Decision tree analysis

State of the world	Probability	NPV	NPV × probability
Boom	0.25	1,249	312.25
Neutral	0.50	258	129
Recession	0.25	(870)	(217.5)
		ENPV	223.75

Clearly, the decision should be that the project is accepted, it having an expected NPV of £232.75.

Theoretically, ENPV cannot be said to take account of risk. This is because it only provides a measure of the expected results of the investment, whereas risk is concerned with the possibility that actual performance and expected performance may not be one and the same. Expected NPV does appeal to management because in an uncertain world, it provides an average value of the performance of the investment in question.

It is important to recognise that the ENPV figure is what management can expect on average. For a specific project the NPV will turn out to be either 312.25, 129 or −217.5 depending upon the economic climate. The average NPV is really only relevant if management is anticipating undertaking a large number of similar investment projects.

Decision Tree Analysis

Decision tree analysis is used by managers when they are faced with a choice between one or more alternative courses of action with the possibility of further alternative courses of action in the future, depending, of course, on which choices were originally made. Decision trees present these choices in diagrammatic form, presenting basic information in a clear and helpful way.

At each point of decision on the tree, probabilities of success and failure are assigned. By multiplying all the probabilities along any route from its origin to its completion, the expected return of each course of action can be found. These alternatives can then be ranked so as to be able to choose the most profitable course of action.

Let us use an example to show how this might work in

Investment appraisal

practice. Antheston Ltd produce a watch which is reaching the decline stage of its product life cycle. Management are faced with three basic options. The first is to withdraw the product and not try to replace it. The second option is to continue with the product as it is and maintain the same financial commitment to it. The third option is to revamp the product itself which will give it a future. The first option, option A, will cost £40,000 in write-off costs; option B will cost £70,000; and option C will cost £200,000. The probability of 'failure' in profit terms for option 'A' is obviously 100%. The probability of option B (keeping things as they are essentially) being successful (ie returning a profit) is only 50%, while the probability of option C being successful is assessed as being 70%. The payoffs for each course of action are shown below. These figures represent the NPVs of the investment over their remaining working life.

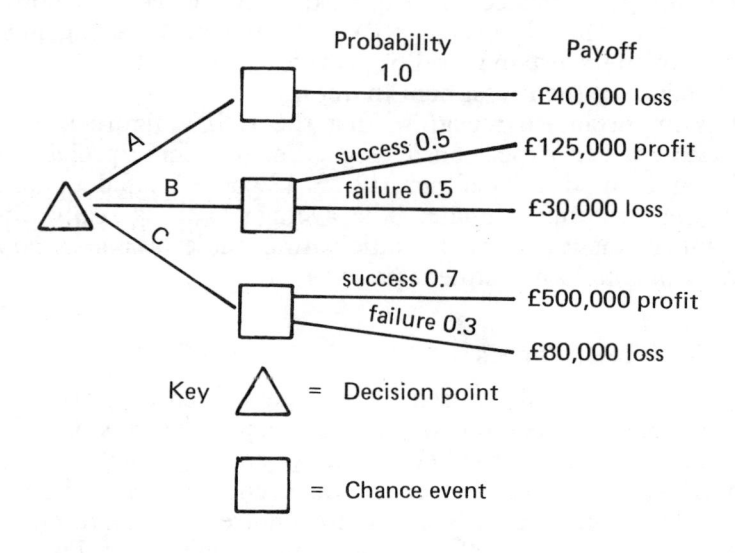

```
                      Probability           Payoff
                         1.0
                     ┌─────┐────────── £40,000 loss
            A       /
                   /    success 0.5 ── £125,000 profit
             B    ┌─────┐
          ──<────  failure 0.5 ─────── £30,000 loss
             C    \
                   \
                    \ success 0.7 ──── £500,000 profit
                    ┌─────┐
                     failure 0.3 ───── £80,000 loss

    Key    △  = Decision point

           □  = Chance event
```

Figure 5.2 Decision tree

The expected money value for each option is now calculated.

Option A = £(40,000)
Option B (0.5×125,000)−(0.5×30,000) = £47,500
Option C (0.7×500,000)−(0.3×80,000) = £326,000

Decision tree analysis

It is clear from this analysis that revamping the product (option C) is by far the most attractive option.

It will be remembered that risk is minimised by diversification. In other words, if Atheston Ltd were a large company and the watchmaking part we have discussed was only a part of their interests, then the 30% chance of the investment making a loss would probably be acceptable. Failure of the investment would not financially endanger the whole company. If the investment discussed were a major part of the business, then failure of the investment might be so destructive as to make option C a foolhardy project. Of course, the example we have used was simple yet, in essence, more complicated decisions or series of decisions can be assessed in exactly the same way. Decision tree analysis does not provide managers with a primary technique for assessing the role of risk in investment appraisal. What it does do is present information in a logical order and help to show managers the likely consequences of the decisions they make, and thus help the decision-making process.

The following is a more complex example. The management of Sashund Ltd are considering undertaking an investment project. Based on their extensive experience they have made two estimates of the cash flow which may arise in each year, along with the probability of each arising. Using an appropriate discount factor they have calculated the present value of each cash flow as shown below.

Year	PV of optimistic cash flow estimate £	Estimated probability	PV of pessimistic cash flow estimate £	Estimated probability
0	(2,500)	0.3	(3,000)	0.7
1	1,200	0.4	1,100	0.6
2	1,500	0.5	1,400	0.5
3	1,000	0.4	800	0.6

Thus whatever the cash flow in year zero, there is a 0.4 chance of a present value cash flow of 1,200 in year one and a 0.6 chance of a cash flow of 1,100 etc. This information can be shown on a decision tree. Probabilities are shown next to lines and present values are shown next to squares (which indicate a chance event). There are two approaches to dealing with decision trees. The first is to establish the outcome for any branch and the

Investment appraisal

probability of that branch. The summation of the EV for each branch gives the total EV shown on Decision Tree I. The other approach is shown in Decision Tree II; having drawn the decision tree we start from the right-hand end and calculate the ENPV at each of the chance events. For example, starting at the top right chance event, ENPV is calculated as follows:

$$(1{,}000 \times 0.4) + (800 \times 0.6) + 1{,}500 = 2{,}380$$

and for the next chance event down:

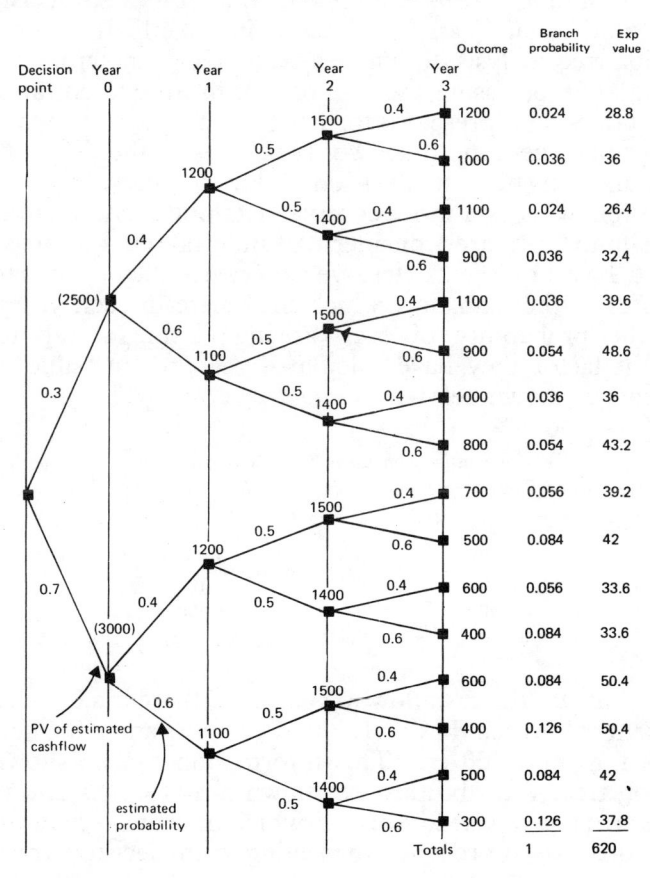

$$(1{,}000 \times 0.4) + (800 \times 0.6) + 1{,}400 = 2{,}280$$

Outcome	Branch probability	Exp value
1200	0.024	28.8
1000	0.036	36
1100	0.024	26.4
900	0.036	32.4
1100	0.036	39.6
900	0.054	48.6
1000	0.036	36
800	0.054	43.2
700	0.056	39.2
500	0.084	42
600	0.056	33.6
400	0.084	33.6
600	0.084	50.4
400	0.126	50.4
500	0.084	42
300	0.126	37.8
Totals	1	620

Figure 5.3 Decision Tree I

Decision tree analysis

These figures are shown circled in between the forks of each chance event.

Having calculated all the ENPVs in that column, we use these values to calculate the ENPVs of the chance events in the next column left. Hence for the uppermost chance event in the second column from the right:

$$\text{ENPV} = (2{,}380 \times 0.5) + (2{,}280 \times 0.5) + 1{,}200 = 3{,}530$$

By continuing this process we eventually derive the ENPV for the project as a whole. In this case it is 620 – a positive ENPV, so the project should be undertaken.

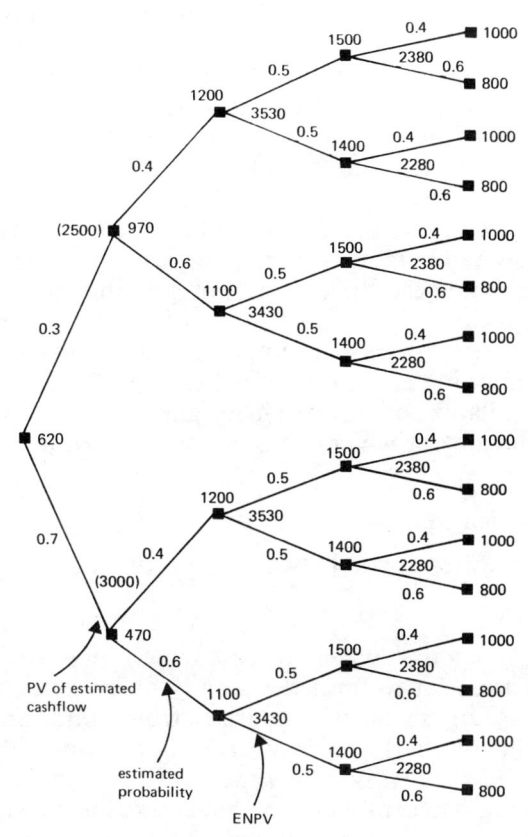

Figure 5.4 Complex decision tree II

6.
Capital Rationing

Up to now, it has been assumed that unlimited funds for investment are always available, and that the only consideration relating to the choice of investments is whether or not they have a positive NPV. This has been based on the perfect capital market model, where loans are always available and at a constant rate of interest. The result of making this basic assumption was that we were able to rule that any investment which had a positive NPV was worthwhile because it would increase the value of the firm for its shareholders, and funds could always be raised to finance the investment.

In practice, however, there is a limit to the amount of funds that a firm is able to borrow – in other words, capital is rationed. In such circumstances, then, it is not possible to pursue all investment options which have a positive NPV. Before we examine investment appraisal in imperfect capital markets where such capital rationing exists (that is where only limited amounts of funds are available and where a firm cannot borrow as much as it wishes) let us look at why capital rationing occurs.

Hard and Soft Rationing

A distinction is often made between these two causes of capital rationing.

Hard rationing occurs when forces which are beyond the company's control act to limit the supply of investment capital available to it. This most usually arises from conditions in the capital market or perhaps even the imposition of central government control. It is sometimes referred to as external capital rationing. Recent surveys have tended to show that industry does not suffer from a shortage of funds for borrowing. When investment has been at historically low levels, it has been demonstrated that this has been because there were few attractive investment options, and not because funds were lacking. This has led Lumby, in *Investment Appraisal* (1984), to observe that hard capital rationing 'is probably of little importance in practice'.

Soft rationing occurs when a company's management impose financial constraints of their own volition. This may be because management wish the company to expand at a steady rate rather than have an excessive growth rate or one which fluctuates from year to year (possibly because the company lacks sufficient staff with adequate skills to be able to cope with an excessive rate of growth). Whatever the formal reason, the major underlying factor will always be a desire to avoid the problems (mainly based on cash flows) caused by a rate of expansion.

Single-period Capital Rationing

This is the simplest form of capital rationing and comes about when financial limits to investment are imposed for a single period only. The investment appraisal problem here is a simple one. The objective is, as always, to implement the most profitable investment, or combination of investments. The solution is to grade all the investment options and implement the most profitable until the cut-off point is reached where the available supply of capital is exhausted.

As ever, NPV is the basis of assessment. The straightforward NPV method cannot itself be used as it stands, instead a benefit-cost ratio, or profitability index, is used. This is found simply by dividing the NPV of future cash flows by the NPV of the total capital outgoings to give the NPV per £1 of investment:

$$\text{Benefit cost ratio} = \frac{\text{NPV future cash flows}}{\text{NPV capital outlay}}$$

In a situation free from capital rationing, all projects with a positive or zero rating would be accepted. Under capital rationing the most profitable investments are those with the highest benefit-cost ratios. Projects should be accepted working down through the rankings of benefit-cost ratios until all the available capital has been used.

Investment appraisal

To illustrate this, let us take an example. Suppose Moxon Ltd have an investment ceiling of £100,000, but four viable investment options open to them in total easily exceed this limit. The four options are independent of each other; that is to say one is not a substitute for another and the success of one option will not militate against the success of another. Suppose also that the projects are divisible, so that in the absence of funds to undertake the whole project, a smaller part of that project may be accepted instead. The cost of capital of 10% and, for the purposes of simplification, inflation and taxation are ignored. The following table shows the outlay and returns from each investment option.

Project	Year 0	Year 1	Year 2	Year 3	Year 4
	£	£	£	£	£
A	(19,000)	9,000	8,000	8,000	3,000
B	(45,945)	22,000	20,000	11,000	10,000
C	(55,909)	25,000	21,200	16,000	12,000
D	(38,000)	16,000	13,000	10,000	10,000

The next step is to calcualte the NPV for each investment option. This is calculated in the normal way. The calculations for option C are, for example:

$$\frac{25,000}{1.1} + \frac{21,200}{1.1^2} + \frac{16,000}{1.1^3} + \frac{12,000}{1.1^4} = 60,465$$

$$60,465 - 55,909 = 4,556$$

so, the NPV of option C is £4,556.

NPV	£
A	3,846
B	5,664
C	4,556
D	1,622

The benefit-cost ratio is then worked out. In the case of option C, the calculation is,

$$\frac{4,556}{55,909} = 0.0815$$

Single-period capital rationing

Cost-benefit ratios:

A	0.2024
B	0.1233
C	0.0815
D	0.0427

Were *NPV* to be used in its simple form to rank the alternatives, the investment strategy would be as follows:

Project	NPV £	Capital required £
B	5,664	45,945
96.7% of C	4,405	54,055
	10,069	100,000

If on the other hand, the *benefit-cost ratio* is used to create an investment strategy, the following selection would result:

Project	NPV £	Capital required £
A	3,846	19,000
B	5,664	45,945
62.7% of C	2,856	35,055
	12,366	100,000

It can be seen, then, that under single-period capital rationing, benefit-cost ratio analysis is superior to straightforward NPV analysis. This is because NPV, in its simple form, takes no account of the amount of capital needed to achieve the return. In the example, using benefit-cost analysis increased NPV returns by £2,303 compared to simple NPV analysis.

Investment appraisal

When Investments are Mutually Exclusive

Benefit-cost analysis can still be used in this situation. The solution, when faced with the prospect of options B and C being mutually exclusive, is to rank the alternatives twice. This is done once with option B excluded, and once with option C excluded. The calculations are shown below. Projects may be mutually exclusive if, for example, there are two alternatives to solving the same problem. Thus, if one wished to export oil, one would either buy a tanker or build a pipeline: one would not do both.

Project	NPV £	Capital required £
A	3,846	19,000
C	4,556	55,909
66% of D	1,071	25,091
	9,473	100,000

Project	NPV £	Capital required £
A	3,846	19,000
B	5,664	45,945
92.25% of D	1,496	35,055
	11,006	100,000

Thus, the optimal investment strategy when B and C are mutually exclusive, is A, B and 92.25% of D.

Multi-period Capital Rationing

So far we have assumed that the company faces a situation of capital rationing only for the duration of a single period. In practice it is much more likely that the supply of capital for investment will be limited for more than one period. In other

Linear programming and investment strategy

words the company will normally have to make investment decisions under a condition of multi-period capital rationing. In this situation the benefit-cost analysis technique cannot be used to identify the optimal investment strategy as it is only applicable when there is a single constraint. Under multi-period capital rationing there will be at least as many constraints as there are years during which capital is restricted. As the number of alternative projects and the number of periods during which capital is restricted increases, the decision process becomes increasingly complex. Therefore under multi-period capital rationing the mathematical technique of *linear programming* is used to identify the optimum strategy.

Linear Programming and Investment Strategy

In developing a lienar programming model we are attempting to summarise the problem faced by the decision-maker into a mathematical model consisting of a number of equations. This model can then be used to 'solve' the problem – that is, to identify the optimal solution which will achieve the decision-maker's objectives.

The use of linear programming in tackling the multi-period capital rationing problem can be best demonstrated using an example.

Investment project – annual outlay (£000)

Year	A	B	C	D	E	F
1	(24)	(108)	(12)	(12)	(60)	(12)
2	(6)	(20)	(12)	(4)	(70)	(20)
3	(10)	(8)	(12)	(10)	(20)	(8)
NPV of project	28	60	34	30	80	12

Since all projects have a positive NPV they would all increase shareholder wealth and therefore should all be undertaken if there was not capital rationing. However, the maximum investment which can be undertaken in each of the three years is as follows:

Investment appraisal

Year	Maximum investment (£000)
1	70
2	40
3	40

The objective of the decision-maker will be to maximise the NPV given the constraints on the availability of capital. We can develop a linear programming model to help the decision-maker to identify the optimal solution, as long as the following assumptions are made:

1. Divisibility, ie we can undertake a certain proportion of a project, for example we could undertake half or two-thirds of a project.

2. Constant returns to scale, ie if we undertake half of a project the returns will be exactly half the predicted NPV for the project in its entirety.

3. Certainty, ie the forecasts of cash flows and NPV, and the relationships between variables are known with certainty.

Having assumed divisibility and constant returns to scale, the total NPV will depend upon the proportion of each project undertaken. If we let the term 'a' represent the proportion of project A which is undertaken, then the NPV generated by undertaking proportion 'a' will be 28a. Similarly the NPV generated from undertaking a given proportion 'b' of project B will be 60b etc. We can therefore say that the objective is to maximise the expression:

$$28a + 60b + 34c + 30d + 80e + 12f$$

The values of a, b, c, d, e and f must lie between zero and one. Zero means the particular project is not undertaken at all, one means that the particular project is undertaken in its entirety.

Having determined the objective function we must now recognise the constraints caused by capital rationing. In year one we cannot invest more than £70,000.

The total investment actually undertaken in year 1 will depend upon the proportion of each individual project that is accepted.

Linear programming and investment strategy

Therefore the total investment in year one will be given by the formula:

$$24a + 108b + 12c + 12d + 60e + 12f$$

but this amount cannot exceed £70,000, so

$$24a + 108b + 12c + 12d + 60e + 12f \leq 70$$

This expression represents the constraint imposed by capital rationing in year one. By exactly the same logic we can establish the constraint expression caused by capital rationing in years two and three:

$$6a + 12b + 12c + 4d + 70e + 20f \leq 40$$

$$10a + 8b + 12c + 10d + 20e + 8f \leq 40$$

The constraint expressions show that the total investment in a given year must be equal to *or less than* the maximum budgeted amount allowed for the year. Therefore we may find that the optimal solution might result in some surplus or 'unused' investment capital in any given year. This surplus can be referred to as 'slack' and can be represented by the letter 'S'. Therefore the value of S (the slack in year one), could in theory be anything from zero (if all £70,000 was invested) to £70,000 (if no investment was undertaken that year).

Using these 'slack' variables we can turn the constraint expressions given above into equations:

$$24a + 108b + 12c + 12d + 60e + 12f + S_1 = 70$$

$$6a + 20b + 12c + 4d + 70e + 20f + S_2 = 40$$

$$10a + 8b + 12c + 10d + 20e + 8f + S_3 = 40$$

We can now formulate the linear programming mode, as follows:

Objective function:
Maximise $28a + 60b + 34c + 30d + 80e + 12f$

Investment appraisal

Subject to the following constraints

$24a + 108b + 12c + 12d + 60e + 12f + S_1 = 70$

$6a + 20b + 12c + 4d + 70e + 20f + S_2 = 40$

$10a + 8b + 12c + 10d + 20e + 8f + S_3 = 40$

There are various methods of solving this model, including manual techniques such as the 'Simplex' method. However, it is highly probable that in practice linear programming problems will be much more complex than the above example and therefore will nearly always be solved using a computer. For this reason the technicalities of manually solving a linear programming problem will not be included here.

Running the problem described above through a computer produces the following data:

Optimum values: $a = 1.00$
$b = 0.07$
$c = 1.00$
$d = 1.00$
$e = 0.235$
$f = 0.00$
$SP_1 = 0.408$
$SP_2 = 0.792$
$SP_3 = 0.00$
Objective function = £115.00

These data now have to be interpreted. The values of a–f represent the proportion of those respective projects which should be undertaken. Therefore projects A, C and D should be fully undertaken; 7% of project B should be undertaken, along with 23.5% of project E. Project F should be totally avoided. Following this strategy will produce the maximum possible NPV of £115,000. SP_1, SP_2 and SP_3 are the 'shadow prices'. These represent the amount by which the value of the objective function would increase (decrease) if one more (less) unit of the binding constraint were available. The value of SP_1 is 0.408, so for every £1000 additional capital which became available in year one, we could increase the overall NPV by £408. Similarly, for each additional £1000 available in year two we could increase

Linear programming and investment strategy

NPV by £792. The value of SP_3 is zero. This indicates that we have not used all the available capital in year three (and therefore we could not increase NPV further by having more capital).

Linear programming is clearly an extremely useful tool in investment appraisal under multi-period capital rationing, particularly when solved by computer. However, we should look more closely at some of the underlying assumptions. First of all we have assumed that projects are divisible, so that we can accept part of a project. In practice this will not always be the case. It is far more likely that we will either have to accept a project in its entirety or not at all. However, a variation of linear programming known as *integer programming* can be used. This works on the basis that a project cannot be partly accepted, in which case the values of a, b, c, etc in the previous example would all have to be either one or zero.

A second assumption, that of constant returns to scale, is also questionable. Certain projects will be divisible to some extent, but it is highly unlikely that the resulting NPV will be an exact proportion of the extent to which the project is undertaken.

A third debatable assumption is that all cash flows and constraints are known with certainty. As time progresses, new opportunities will present themselves and circumstances will change, thereby invalidating previous assumptions regarding cash flows and constraints. Having said this, it is of course inevitable that assumptions as to future constraints and cash flows have to be made, but it is essential that management recognise their fallibility in making predictions in a world of uncertainty, and that they use linear programming as an aid to decision making. The results of a linear programming exercise should not be treated as gospel simply because they have been produced by a computer.

7.
Applications of Investment Appraisal

Up to this point, investment appraisal has largely been discussed and explained in terms of that ideal state of the world where no inflation or taxation exist. Thus we have been able to assume that £1 today has the same purchasing power as £1 a year or even five years from today. As we all know, inflation, at whatever percentage rate, is a fact of life. Inflation erodes purchasing power, creates uncertainty as to the real value of estimated future incomes, and creates problems when trying to price products. We will look first, then, at how inflation affects investment appraisal and decision-making, and how appraisal techniques can be modified to cope with price changes.

Inflation

Inflation can be defined as an increase in the general price level. The presence of inflation will ensure that the preference of the individual for early consumption is increased. The longer he waits and defers consumption, the less purchasing power his money will have. To get around this problem, the lender of funds will wish to take inflation into account when making investment decisions.

The investor will continue to use the NPV method but will discount cash flows by using a discount rate which allows for inflation. Thus, the investor's time value of money will be combined with the inflation factor so that high levels of inflation do not nullify his investment.

To take an example, suppose Jack Watt Ltd wish to invest £1,000. Their cost of capital is 10% and inflation is running at 8%. If this investment were merely to break even, Jack Watt Ltd would want £1,188 at the end of year one (assuming that the investment was to run for only one year). This is because the money rate of interest, or marginal rate of time preference as it is

Inflation

also known, is equal to 18.8%. This was found by multiplying the percentage cost of capital with the percentage inflation rate:

$$(1+0.10)(1+0.08)$$
$$= 1.10 \times 1.08$$
$$= 1.188 \text{ or } 18.8\%$$

To put the above example in a slightly different form, if no inflation existed the investment would need to yield £100 to make a £1,100 return. This £1,100 would buy the same amount of goods and services as £1,188 at a time of 8% inflation:

$$\frac{1188}{1.08} = 1,100$$

The return of 10% is known as the real rate of interest. We can now describe the return on the investment using the expression:

$$1000 = \frac{1188}{1.188} = \frac{1188}{(1.08)(1.10)}$$

The denominators show that one plus the money rate of interest equals one plus the inflation rate multiplied by the real rate of interest.

$$(1+m) = (1+i)(1+r)$$

where

m = money rate of interest
i = inflation rate
r = real rate of interest

To show how this would work in practice, let us suppose that Jack Watt Ltd invested £1,000, that its cost of capital was again 10% and inflation was running at 8%. The project had a life of four years and, bearing inflation in mind, the nominal cash flows were estimated to be £450 in year one, £425 in year two and £400 in years three and four. The calculation would be,

Investment appraisal

$$\text{NPV} = \frac{450}{1.188} + \frac{425}{1.188} + \frac{400}{1.188} + \frac{400}{1.188} - 100$$

NPV = £119.30

NPV indicates that the investment increases the value of the firm and is, in consequence, worth undertaking.

An alternative way of dealing with inflation in discounting is to forecast the cash flows in money terms, allowing for the effects of inflation, and then to convert these figures into real terms by discounting at the inflation rate. This restates the cash flows in constant purchasing power terms. These 'real' cash flows can then be discounted by the real discount rate to get the NPV.

Year	'Money' cash flow £	Inflation discount £	'Real' cash flow £	Real interest rate discount %	Present value £
0	(1,000)	1,000	(1,000)	1.000	(1,000)
1	450	0.926	416.67	0.909	378.75
2	425	0.857	364.37	0.826	300.97
3	400	0.794	317.53	0.751	238.47
4	400	0.735	294.01	0.683	200.80
					118.99

This is sprecisely the result found earlier (allowing for rounding errors).

So far, we have assumed that inflation is general in its effects: an inflation rate of 8% has been assumed to increase all individual prices by 8%. This assumption is, of course, unrealistic. Inflation is calculated by monitoring the price increases of a basket of goods for an average household. Within that basket, some prices will increase by more than the average; some less. Furthermore, this basket of goods may not be a relevant guide for a business. Businesses may then have to use price level indices calculated for various business sectors, or they may have to find the different inflation rates as they apply to income and expenditure.

Let us now assume that the cash inflows and outflows associated with a project are *not* affected in exactly the same way

Inflation

by inflation, so that there are relative price movements. For example, in appraising the following project the directors of Mornybe Ltd initially ignore inflation. They estimate that the cash inflow in the current year will be £30,000 and the expenses incurred to achieve this inflow will be £15,000 (giving a net cash inflow of £15,000 during the current year). The physical volume of output and input is expected to remain constant for the next five years, but the sales price will increase by 5% per annum and the cost of sales will increase by 12% per annum.

The directors, therefore, must calculate the net cash flow in money terms for each year.

Year	Sales (5% inflation) £	Cost of sales (12% inflation) £	Net cash flow £
1	=30,000	=15,000	15,000
2	30,000×1.05=31,500	15,000×1.12=16,800	14,700
3	31,500×1.05=33,075	16,800×1.12=18,816	14,259
4	33,075×1.05=34,729	18,816×1.12=21,074	13,655
5	34,729×1.05=36,465	21,074×1.12=23,603	12,862

Having calculated the money cash flow for each year, allowing for the relative price movement, the directors of Mornybe must now deflate these cash flows in order to express their unit current purchasing power terms. The resulting figures are known as the 'net current cost cash flow' (or NCCF). The directors decide to use the Retail Price Index (RPI) as a deflator which we shall assume is increasing at 10% per annum. Once the NCCF has been established these values can be discounted at the real cost of capital (15%) in order to establish the present values of the cash flow.

Net money cash flow £	Deflator (10%)	Net current cost cash flow £	Discount factor (15%)	Present value £
15,000	1,000	15,000	1.000	15,000
14,700	0.909	13,362	0.870	11,619
14,259	0.826	11,778	0.756	8,904
13,655	0.751	10,255	0.658	6,748
12,862	0.683	8,785	0.552	4,849
				47,120

Investment appraisal

Therefore relative price movements must be dealt with in the following manner:

1. Inflate each component element of the project at the appropriate rate.
2. Calculate the net *money* cash flow.
3. Deflate the net money cash flows in order to express them in current cost terms. The RPI can be used as an index of general price movements, but where possible a more specific price index should be used (many large firms calculate their own price index). This gives the net current cost cash flow.
4. Discount the net current cost cash flow at the *real* cost of capital in order to derive the present value of these cash flows.

Stages 3 and 4 will be combined if the cost of capital is expressed as a nominal or money cost of capital.

Inflation and the Cost of Borrowing

An important effect of inflation is its impact on borrowed funds. Inflation has the effect of reducing the real cost of borrowing; its significance when making investments is plain.

An example will readily illustrate the point. If Salmon Ltd borrow £100 for one year at an interest rate of 10% when inflation is at 0%, then the amount repaid is £100 plus £10 in interest making a total of £110. If however the level of inflation is 5% during the year, then the amount paid back in real terms is only £104.76.

$$110 \times \frac{1}{1.05} = 104.76$$

or £6.24 less. Had inflation been running at over 10%, there would have been no borrowing costs in real terms.

In summary, it appears that inflation does not present insurmountable problems to investment appraisal. The real problem is in the prediction of future levels of inflation. Treasury forecasts generally provide accurate information for the near future; that is up to a year ahead (or two at the most). In an uncertain world, any predictions of inflation rates into the more distant future are only educated guesses, as likely to be inaccurate as accurate. For the purposes of investment appraisal, such educated guesses have to be made. It serves as one more reminder that accounting disciplines can never become an exact science.

Taxation

Taxation is a vital element to be considered when examining the cash flows of a potential investment. Investments are carried out, in essence, to increase and maximise shareholder wealth. Shareholder wealth in turn is maximised at the after-tax level. Thus, for the purposes of investment appraisal, the manager is concerned with the after-tax cash flows of an investment.

Before going on to look at how taxation affects investment appraisal, it is wise to remember that the tax system is not an unchanging structure. Fundamental changes (in so far as they have affected investment decision-making) have taken place during the last decade or so. To give a complete description of the tax system as it currently operates would be to tempt fate and fossilize this work before its time. Therefore, this section will attempt to explain the fundamentals of dealing with taxation; to explain taxation in general rather than give a detailed, up-to-the-minute review of corporate taxation.

Taxation has two faces; each of which the manager has to bear in mind. One face is negative: taxes are levied on profits. The positive side is that a network of tax allowances exists which reduces the tax repayments on those profits.

First, let us look at corporation tax, which is the tax levied on company profits. The normal rate of tax is currently 35%, though lower rates apply for 'small' businesses which are defined as those whose profits are below a given figure (£100,000 in 1987). Profit as defined by the Inland Revenue is not the same as that which appears in the firm's profit and loss account. It is an adjusted profit which gives certain allowances and adds certain sums on. Those expenses which are deducted from profit in the profit and loss account but are disallowed for tax purposes include:

Investment appraisal

1. Depreciation charges
2. Entertainment expenses (unless incurred in entertaining overseas customers)
3. Political contributions
4. Provisions for bad debts.

By far the most important of these disallowed items is depreciation charges. Depreciation, although charged against profits as an operating expense in the profit and loss account, is added back to the profit figure by the Inland Revenue. It is disallowed for tax purposes because it is merely a book charge designed to avoid the distortions to profitability which would arise if the purchase price of long-term assets was wholly charged against profits in the year of purchase. There are many alternative methods of calculating depreciation, each of which can result in a quite different depreciation charge. Depreciation is therefore considered to be too subjective and susceptible to manipulation to be allowed as a charge against tax. So, if the company profit as shown in the profit and loss account amounted to £500,000, and the four aforementioned disallowed items totalled £100,000, then the running total so far for taxable profits would be £600,000.

This is not the end of the story, however, as the Inland Revenue will allow the deduction of certain items from taxable profit. These include:

1. stock relief
2. capital allowances

Stock relief is given by the Inland Revenue by, in effect, not taxing that part of the increase in stock values due purely to the effect of inflation. In most cases tax is assessed by referring to a special price index compiled by the Central Statistical Office. Where stock levels are considerable, stock relief is reduced by the proportion of borrowings to total assets. This is because where a firm is highly geared, the lenders of money are bearing the effects of inflation and not the shareholders. Thus, if a firm is geared 80:20, then stock relief will be reduced by one-fifth after taking account of the price index and actual stock levels.

Capital allowances are in effect a standardised method of allowing for depreciation charges on fixed assets thereby avoiding the problems of subjectivity and manipulation referred

Taxation

to earlier. They are also a Treasury tool for encouraging investment. Rates of capital allowance vary for different categories of assets in different industries. Thus industrial buildings will attract different (higher) capital allowances than will hotel buildings, and buildings used by service industries attract no capital allowances. Plant and machinery, and company cars will attract a certain percentage annual allowance (known as a 'writing-down allowance'). The method of capital allowance relief given, for example, on plant and machinery is to grant an annual writing-down allowance which is calculated as a percentage on a reducing balance basis.

To take an example, the directors of Peat Haul (Earth Movers) Ltd, are considering whether to purchase a new excavator which will cost £60,000. In appraising this investment project it is essential that the directors take account of the effects of taxation on the cost of the asset. If we assume that the writing-down allowance for plant and machinery is 25% (as was the case in the 1986 tax year), then in the first year when the machine is purchased, a capital allowance of £15,000 (ie 25% of £60,000) will be granted for the machine. Therefore the purchase of the excavator will reduce the company's taxable profit by £15,000. If we further asume that Peat Haul (Earth Movers) Ltd is a 'large' company for tax purposes (which in the 1986 tax year was defined as one with taxable profits in excess of £500,000) and that the large company tax rate is 35% then the capital allowance will reduce the company's tax bill for the year by £5,250 (35% of £15,000). This figure should be reflected in the cash flow forecasts used to evaluate the investment opportunity. Similar calculations should be made for each year during which the machine will be held by the company.

In addition to calculating the amount of tax involved in a project, it is also essential that the timing of tax payments is taken into account, particularly when calculating present values. Corporation tax is usually payable nine months and one day after the end of the company's accounting period. Consequently the effects of taxation on a project's cash flow will not make a marked impression until anything up to twenty-one months after the purchase of an asset. For example, if Peat Haul (Earth Movers) Ltd have a financial year end of 31 March, then the tax effects of an asset purchase made on 1 April 1986 would not become apparent in cash flow terms until 1 January

Investment appraisal

1988 (ie nine months and one day after the next financial year end).

One final point to make is that when certain assets such as expensive cars or industrial buildings are disposed of a balancing up with the Inland Revenue takes place in order to reflect the fact that the actual cost of using an asset over its lifetime may differ from the cost allowed for by the capital allowances charged over the asset's life.

If a relevant asset is sold for more than its written-down book value then the Inland Revenue has been over-generous in its capital allowances. This situation is corrected by use of a 'balancing charge', which equals the excess of the proceeds of sale over the asset's written-down book value. The total capital allowance claim for the year is reduced by the amount of any balancing charges arising during that year. Conversely, when an asset is sold for an amount less than its book value a balancing allowance is added to the other capital allowances for the year to recognise the fact that the written-down allowances underestimated the true cost of using the asset.

To go back to the example given at the start, taxable profits stand at £600,000. If capital allowances and stock relief come to £150,000, then taxable profits are £450,000. If we assume that corporation tax is levied at 35% on a business of this size, the tax bill will be £157,000.

Companies can thus estimate what impact a particular investment will have on overall profitability, and, allied with a knowledge of tax allowances, will be able to work out how that investment affects tax liabilities, and thus will be able to assess the overall worth of the investment.

Replacement Decisions

At some point the time comes when a firm wishes to replace fixed assets. This is because either at the end of an asset's working life it becomes more costly to run and less efficient or because a new machine has a different capacity.

The manager will need to know how frequently, and when, to replace his fixed assets in order to minimise his costs and thereby maximise profits. He must therefore identify the optimum *replacement cycle*. Factors which must be taken into account when making replacement decisions include:

1. capital costs of the asset
2. operating and maintenance costs
3. residual values
4. opportunity costs
5. cost of capital
6. inflation
7. taxation and investment incentives.

When comparing alternative replacement cycles, or alternative replacements for an existing asset, it is essential that like is compared with like. We cannot directly compare the costs of a three-year cycle with those of a five-year cycle, or the costs of different machines with different expected useful lives. The crucial point in determining the optimum replacement policy is that we *must* consider the cash flows of alternative cycles or machines over equal time periods. We therefore need to compare standardised sets of information in order to achieve a fair comparison. There are two techniques which ensure that a valid comparison is made:

1. the lowest common mutiple method
2. the annual equivalent annuity factor method.

Lowest Common Multiple

This method allows comparison of alternative replacement cycles or assets with different life spans by calculating the lowest common multiple of the possible replacement cycles, and then calculating the NPV of the costs of each of the alternatives over this period.

For example, the directors of Jaynawl Ltd wish to compare the costs of a one-, two-, and three-year replacement cycle. The initial outlay required to purchase a new asset is £10,000. The operating and maintenance costs increase the longer the asset is held, and the residual value (ie the resale value) declines with age. Operating and maintenance costs are known through experience, and the residual values have been established from

Investment appraisal

tables showing the second-hand value of such an asset depending upon age and condition.

Time/age of asset:	t_0	t_1	t_2	t_3
Initial outlay:	(10,000)			
Operating and maintenance cost:		(2,000)	(4,000)	(5,000)
Residual value at end of year:		7,000	5,000	4,000

The lowest common multiple of one, two and three is six. We must therefore calculate the annual cash flows under each replacement cycle over six years.

One-year replacement cycle:

Year	Replacement cost	Operating and maintenance	Residual value	Net cash flow
	£	£	£	£
0	(10,000)			(10,000)
1	(10,000)	(2,000)	7,000	(5,000)
2	(10,000)	(2,000)	7,000	(5,000)
3	(10,000)	(2,000)	7,000	(5,000)
4	(10,000)	(2,000)	7,000	(5,000)
5	(10,000)	(2,000)	7,000	(5,000)
6		(2,000)	7,000	5,000

The above calculation assumes that the old machine is sold and the new one bought exactly at the turn of the year, and that the machine is *not* replaced at the end of year six.

Two-year Replacement Cycle:

Year	Replacement cost	Operating and maintenance	Residual value	Net cash flow
	£	£	£	£
0	(10,000)			(10,000)
1		(2,000)		(2,000)
2	(10,000)	(4,000)	5,000	(9,000)
3		(2,000)		(2,000)
4	(10,000)	(4,000)	5,000	(9,000)
5		(2,000)		(2,000)
6		(4,000)	5,000	1,000

Lowest common multiple

Three-Year Replacement Cycle:

Year	Replacement cost £	Operating and maintenance £	Residual value £	Net cash flow £
0	(10,000)			(10,000)
1		(2,000)		(2,000)
2		(4,000)		(4,000)
3	(10,000)	(5,000)	4,000	(11,000)
4		(2,000)		(2,000)
5		(4,000)		(4,000)
6		(5,000)	4,000	(1,000)

Having calculated the cash flows over the six-year period, the directors of Jaynawl Ltd can calculate the NPV of each of the three alternatives over six years. Jaynawl's cost of capital is 10%.

Year	Discount factor £	One-year cycle cash flow £	PV £	Two-year cycle cash flow £	PV £	Three-year cycle cash flow £	PV £
0	1.000	(10,000)	(10,000)	(10,000)	(10,000)	(10,000)	(10,000)
1	0.909	(5,000)	(4,545)	(2,000)	(1,818)	(2,000)	(1,818)
2	0.826	(5,000)	(4,130)	(9,000)	(7,434)	(4,000)	(3,304)
3	0.751	(5,000)	(3,755)	(2,000)	(1,502)	(11,000)	(8,261)
4	0.683	(5,000)	(3,415)	(9,000)	(6,147)	(2,000)	(1,366)
5	0.621	(5,000)	(3,105)	(2,000)	(1,242)	(1,000)	(2,484)
6	0.565	5,000	2825	1,000	565		(565)
		NPV	26,125		27,578		27,798

Therefore the one-year replacement cycle offers the lowest cost in NPV terms over the six-year period (although this does not tell us exactly when the asset should be replaced).

The great advantage of the lowest common multiple method is that it can cope with relative price movements. In the example above we assumed that prices would stay stable over the six-year period. We can, however, use this method when the replacement cost, operating and maintenance costs and residual values are expected to be affected by different rates of price movements. We would simply inflate each cost element by the appropriate rate in order to determine the actual cash flows in each year.

The drawbacks of the lowest common multiple method

Investment appraisal

include the fact that for assets with lives of five years or more the technique very quickly becomes unwieldy – for example, the lowest common multiple of five- and seven-year replacement cycles is thirty-five years. Apart from the time taken to carry out the analysis, the assumptions that (a) a company would anticipate using the same type of asset for thirty-five years, and (b) that it is possible to forecast cash flows over such a long period, are somewhat unrealistic. Secondly, the lowest common multiple method in its simple form does not lend itself to comparisons between non-identical assets.

Annual Equivalent Annuity

This technique involves forecasting the cash flows for *one* cycle, and calculating the NPV. In order to allow comparison of cycles of different length this NPV is then converted into an annual equivalent annuity which can then be directly compared with that of other replacement cycles.

If the NPV of a ten-year cycle is £1,000 and the NPV of a one-year cycle is £999 it would clearly be wrong to accept the one-year cycle simply because it has a lower NPV, because this is a one-year cycle only. Similarly if a one-year cycle has an NPV of £1,000 and a two-year cycle has an NPV of £2,000 we cannot say the two are the same – it would be better to undertake the one-year cycle and repeat it in a year's time because the NPV of doing this twice is less than undertaking the two-year cycle immediately. The annual equivalent approach deals with this problem by standardising the cost information.

For example, the director of M Overs Van Hire Ltd are trying to identify the optimum replacement cycle which will minimise the costs of operating their vehicles. The relevant data are as follows:

Age of car (years)	1	2	3	4
Replacement cost £7,000				
Annual operating and maintemance cost	500	750	1,000	2,000
Residual value at end of year	4,750	3,500	3,000	2,250

On the basis of this data the cash flow for each replacement cycle can be calculated.

Annual equivalent annuity

One-year Replacement Cycle:

Year	Replacement cost £	Operating and maintenance £	Residual value £	Net cash flow £
0	(7,000)			(7,000)
1		(500)	4,750	4,250

Two-year Replacement Cycle:

Year	Replacement cost £	Operating and maintenance £	Residual value £	Net cash flow £
0	(7,000)			(7,000)
1		(500)		(500)
2		(750)	3,500	2,750

Three-year Replacement Cycle:

Year	Replacement cost £	Operating and maintenance £	Residual value £	Net cash flow £
0	(7,000)			(7,000)
1		(500)		(500)
2		(750)		(750)
3		(1,000)	3,000	2,000

Four-year Replacement Cycle:

Year	Replacement cost £	Operating and maintenance £	Residual value £	Net cash flow £
0	(7,000)			(7,000)
1		(500)		(500)
2		(750)		(750)
3		(1,000)		(1,000)
4		(2,000)	2,250	250

Investment appraisal

Having calculated the cash flows, the directors can determine the NPV of each cycle length. M Overs Van Hire Ltd uses a discount rate of 10%.

Year	Discount Factor	CYCLE LENGTH							
		1 YEAR		2 YEARS		3 YEARS		4 YEARS	
		Cash flow	PV	Cash flow	PV	Cash flow	PV	Cash flow	PV
0	1.000	(7,000)	(7,000)	(7,000)	(7,000)	(7,000)	(7,000)	(7,000)	(7,000)
1	0.909	4,250	3,863	(500)	(455)	(455)	(500)	(500)	(455)
2	0.826			2,750	2,272	(750)	(620)	(750)	(620)
3	0.751					2,000	1,502	(1,000)	(751)
4	0.683							250	171
NPV			(3,137)		(5,183)		(6,573)		(8,655)

The annual equivalent factor is found by adding all the discount factors used in the NPV calculation:

One-year cycle – annual equivalent factor = 0.909
Two-year cycle   0.909+0.826 = 1.735
Three-year cycle   0.909+0.826+0.751 = 2.486
Four-year cycle   0.909+0.826+0.751+0.683 = 3.169

In practice these values would be found from an annual equivalent factor table.

If the asset has an NPV of (5183) over a two-year cycle then the annual equivalent cost is:

$$\frac{(5183)}{1.735} = (2987)$$

In other words, incurring a cost of £2987 in each of the two years has a present value of £5183, which is the same NPV as the asset over a two-year cycle. Thus we can calculate the annual equivalent cost for each length of cycle and choose the lowest.

1 year cycle annual equivalent cost =   3137
2 year cycle annual equivalent cost = $\frac{5183}{1.735}$ = 2987

Annual equivalent annuity

3 year cycle annual equivalent cost = $\dfrac{6573}{2.486}$ = 2644

4 year cycle annual equivalent cost = $\dfrac{8655}{3.169}$ = 2731

Therefore, since the three-year cycle has the lowest annual equivalent cost, M Overs Van Hire Ltd should replace their vans once every three years in order to minimise their costs.

Both the lowest common multiple approach and the annual equivalent cost technique will give the same results, but the annual equivalent technique is often easier to use, particularly when the cycle times involved are more than, say, five years. However, the annual equivalent cost method does not deal quite so well with relative price movements.

The presence of rapid technological change complicates the analysis somewhat, as allowance must be made for the fact that a shorter cycle time may allow easier adaptation of new technology at lower cost.

The effects of taxation should of course be taken into account, and may determine the optimal time to invest in a new asset. For example, if there is a proposed change in the tax laws this may have implications as to when is the best time to buy an asset.

The advantage of using a planned replacement cycle is that it allows for the forward planning of cash flows, creates time to plan for asset replacement, so causing the least amount of bother, and minimises total operating costs. To take an example, Wilt plc are planning to buy a new assembly machine. Though the working life of this machine is limited, an agreement with the manufacturers of the machine ensures that its cost will remain the same for the near future. The machine costs £3,500 and its scrap value and running costs are set below:

	Year 1 £	Year 2 £	Year 3 £	Year 4 £	Year 5 £
Running costs	1,000	1,375	1,750	2,000	2,300
Scrap value	2,000	1,500	1,000	250	—

For the purposes of simplicity, taxation and inflation are ignored. Wilt plc have a cost of capital of 10%.

Investment appraisal

The equivalent annual costs of keeping the machine are set out below:

Year	Scrap value £	Running costs £	PV of SV £	PV of RC £	NPV £	10% factor £	Equivalent annual cost £
1	2,000	1,000	1,818	909	2,591	0.9091	2,850
2	1,500	1,375	1,240	1,136	4,305	1.7355	2,481
3	1,000	1,750	751	1,315	6,109	2.4869	2,456
4	250	2,000	171	1,366	8,055	3.1699	2,541

From the figures, then, it is apparent that the assembly machine should be replaced every three years.

Lease or Buy Decisions

It is difficult to categorise leasing. However, two broad categories are frequently used:

1. Operating leases which can be described as rental agreements normally between the user of the equipment (the lessee) and the supplier (the lessor). The lessor is responsible for service and maintenance. The period of the lease is less than the economic life. The lessor will at the end of the agreement be in a position to lease the asset to another party.

2. Financial leases are agreements normally between the user of the equipment (the lessee) and a finance house or similar (the lessor). In this case the lessee is responsible for the upkeep of the equipment. The primary period of the agreement covers the bulk of the asset's useful life. Thereafter the asset may be further leased for a small annual fee or sold with proceeds split between parties according to the terms of the agreement.

The essence of a lease or buy decision is that different cash flows over time need to be compared. Again, there is a clear case of using the NPV system method.

To take an example, Cutzee Ltd need a van to distribute their product and are faced with either leasing or buying the van. The van can be leased for the four-year period at £5,000 per annum. The maintenance and service costs are included in the price.

Lease or buy decisions

Alternatively the van can be bought for £12,000 and at the end of four years its residual value will be £2,000. The service and maintenance costs are estimated to be £1,000 per year. The company's cost of borrowing is 12%.

The cost of buying is as follows:

Year	Discount factor	Purchase £	PV £	Maintenance £	PV £	Scrap £	PV £
0	1.000	(12,000)	(12,000)				
1	0.8979			(1,000)	(893)		
2	0.7972			(1,000)	(797)		
3	0.7118			(1,000)	(712)		
4	0.6335			(1,000)	(637)	2,000	1,271

NPV = (£13,767) = 1,271 − 12,000 − 3,038

The cost of leasing is:

Year	Discount factor	Cash flow £	PV £
1	0.8979	(5,000)	(4,465)
2	0.7972	(5,000)	(3,986)
3	0.7118	(5,000)	(3,559)
4	0.6355	(5,000)	(3,178)

NPV = (£15,187)

The decision to buy rather than lease, seems clear.

A closer examination of the leasing decisions involves a number of complexities:

1. Which discount rate should be used? The traditional argument is that the oportunity cost should be used. The normal assumption is that the leasing arrangement replaces the need to borrow; consequently borrowing costs are a reflection of opportunity costs.

2. What has happened to the original decision of whether the van was worth while? The traditional approach is essentially twofold:

   (a) The cash flows associated with the asset are discounted

Investment appraisal

using the weighted average cost of capital (WACC) – to cope with the uncertainty of cash flows.
(b) Once a positive NPV indicates acquisition is justified, the alternative financing cash flows are discounted by the cost of borrowing to establish the cheapest financing arrangement. The bank rate is used because the financing cash flows are known with a high degree of certainty.

In both cases the after-tax rates should be used.

The disadvantage of the traditional approach is that it may reject investments without taking into account the cheapest method of financing. A solution would be to establish the cheapest financing arrangement first. The costs of the finance are then subtracted from the positive cash flows associated with the acquisition decision.

3. Should lessors discount at the same rate as lessees? It is frequently assumed that leasing companies are financial intermediaries and so able to gain access to funds at a lower cost than the lessee. This indicates a difference in discount rates, which may be reinforced by differences in the marginal rate of corporation tax of the two parties. In practice the lessor faces risks of non payment and poor residual values, consequently the differences in rate of discount might be slight.

A study published in 1979 carried out by C R Tomkins, J F Lower and E J Morgan into an economic analysis of leasing, concluded that the leasing decision involves many factors and is more complex than comparing the cash flows of the alternatives. These factors include inadequate access to alternative sources of finance, problems of maintaining sophisticated equipment, technical obsolescence and the changing nature of the tax system.

8.
Investment Appraisal in the Public Sector

The preceding discussion of investment appraisal has been based on the premise that the decision-maker is operating in the private sector and is primarily concerned with profit maximisation. Consequently, the investment appraisal techniques which have been described are aimed at identifying those projects which will help achieve the objective of maximisation of private wealth. They therefore take account only of the *private* costs and returns of capital projects, ie those which accrue directly to the investor. There are, however, many instances where the private costs and benefits of a project do not reflect the true *social* costs and benefits. For example, an appraisal of a proposed chemical plant will consider the investment which is required in order to build the plant, the cost of raw materials, labour costs etc, and the revenues which are expected to arise from the operation of the proposed plant. However, no account will be taken of the wider social and environmental consequences of building the plant. These include the beneficial effects of, say, increased employment if the plant is to be built in a depressed area, the effect on the balance of trade if the products will be exported, and the detrimental effects such as environmental pollution, damage to the local scenery, the effect on local house prices etc.

When appraising investments from a social point of view, such as a proposed new motorway or hydro-electric scheme, the investment appraisal techniques developed for use in the private sector are inadequate. It becomes necessary to use a technique which takes a much broader view of costs and benefits. Cost-benefit analysis (CBA) is one such investment appraisal technique for analysing and measuring the costs and benefits to society of proposed investments. CBA is concerned with maximising not private profit, but the overall welfare of a defined society. It therefore seeks to take account of not only the direct tangible costs and revenues associated with a given project but

Investment appraisal

also the intangible costs and benefits to society as a whole. It therefore classifies costs and benefits in a different way to private sector investment appraisal. For example, if the management of a factory decide (or are forced by legislation) to install pollution control equipment, this represents a cost to the company but a benefit to society. CBA is widely used in the public sector in appraising investment projects.

CBA can be developed from two standards of economic thought. These are public goods – theory of externalities – and investment appraisal techniques.

1. Public Goods, Externalities

Many economic activities are provided inadequately by a market system because they exhibit public good characteristics or simply because they generate external benefits or costs. Public goods are those from which people cannot be excluded if they refuse to pay and which are not depleted even if they are consumed by a number of individuals, eg army, police. Clearly the individual or household will tend to under-reveal his preferences for such goods – he will not make voluntary payments for enjoying them if he cannot be excluded from consuming them, he will be a *free-rider*. In other words he will enjoy the benefit of consumption of such goods without having to pay for the privilege of doing so. Because it is impossible to exclude people from consumption of a 'public' good, no rational private sector company will provide such goods because it is impossible to collect revenues from consumers. Public goods, such as national defence or law and order must therefore be the concern of the public sector which is responsible for deciding: (a) whether they should be produced at all, and (b) if so, in what quantities. Cost-benefit analysis is a technique for helping to make such decisions. It is an economic technique in that it attempts to relate social costs to social benefits, so recognising the basic economic problem of *choice* in the use of scarce resources. (Alternative decision-making techniques here would be voting, traditional customs etc.)

Similar to public goods are externalities where the production or consumption of goods and services may generate costs (eg pollution) or benefits (eg good architecture) for parties who are not directly involved in the transaction. Hence the market prices which reflect private costs and benefits are an inappropriate indicator of the true social cost, and the external or spillover or neighbourhood effects must be additionally taken into account in the decision-making process so that social rather than private welfare is evaluated. Again cost-benefit analysis may be used where such goods are provided by the public sector, or in certain cases (eg transport) it may be used in the private sector. Cost-benefit analysis attempts to take into account all the costs and benefits of a particular decision and not just those that are particular to the individual decision-makers – ie social flows not just financial flows. The equivalent private (financial) and public (social) flows can be demonstrated as follows:

Private benefit *or* revenue	– Social benefit *or* private benefit plus external effects
Private cost *or* cash outlays	– Social cost *or* private cost plus external effects
Profit	Net social benefit

2. Investment Appraisal

Most projects for which cost-benefit analysis is used involve costs and benefits which arise over a number of years (eg a road widening scheme). Because of this it is necesary to use investment appraisal techniques which evaluate future costs and benefits in present value terms. The two main methods are net present value and yield, which are easily adapted to social cost-benefit analysis since the major difference between financial investment appraisal and CBA is simply the broader definition which the latter gives to the meaning of 'costs' and 'benefits'.

Cost-benefit analysis is a technique for aiding the choice between competing projects in the public sector . . . it defines 'costs' and 'benefits' very broadly and uses or adapts traditional investment-appraisal techniques to its needs.

Investment appraisal

The Stages in a Cost-benefit Study

1. *Which costs and benefits to include?*

Cost-benefit analysis would attempt to include all the costs and benefits of a particular project in an ideal situation. For example, if a road widening scheme is envisaged then not only will the money costs of paying the contractors be included but also an attempt would be made to include the environmental damage (or improvement) such as visual damage or noise levels on the surrounding area. There are certain things which must be dealt with cautiously in this stage of the analysis.

(a) *Double-counting* has to be avoided. For example, it would be wrong to include, as a result of the construction of a new road from a commuter town to the main local city, *both* the value in journey time saved to motorists using the road *and* any increase in property values in the commuter town. The latter is caused by the former, so that to include both would be double-counting.

(b) *Elimination of insignificant effects.* The effects of any project are likely to be widespread so that the inclusion of *all* costs and benefits would either be impossible or at least very costly. The effects may be widespread *geographically*, as for example with reduced congestion on alternative routes as a result of the construction of a new motorway. Or, the effects might be widespread in *type*, as for example with a new reservoir which, amongst other things, changes the visual nature of the area, effects recreational activities, and has an influence on the ecology of the area.

Given this wide range of possible effects the cost-benefit analyst must choose which he should include. *This does imply a possibility of bias or simply inaccuracy.*

2. *The Measurement and Evaluation of the Costs and Benefits*

The next stage in the analysis is the measurement of the costs and benefits in terms of physical quantities – eg number of hours saved and fall in the number of serious injuries as a result of a road improvement project. In general this is a relatively straightforward process, but difficulties do arise in the measure-

The stages in a cost-benefit study

ment of *intangibles*, such as 'good taste' in architecture.

A more difficult problem, and one of more interest to the economist, is the evaluation of the costs and benefits. Generally this is done in money terms so that comparisons can easily be made with other similarly evaluated public projects, and also with the private sector. (This is not always the case; the Buchanan Report on 'Traffic in Towns' used an index number system for evaluation.)

Market Prices. In general, it is a good rule of thumb to use market prices where they are available. This would be the case, for example, concerning measuring the construction costs of a road or reservoir project. Here the price paid to the constructor would be the appropriate measure of value. Difficulties do arise in using this mechanism of prices in that the market itself may be imperfect, due to externalities or monopolies for example, in which case the prices might need adjusting.

For most public projects costs are often easy to evaluate in this way, although there are exceptions such as the visual damage an urban motorway might create. Generally, it is on the benefits side of the calculation that most difficulties arise, as in the case of evaluating the effect of reduced congestion on the saving of lives.

Shadow Prices. Where market prices are either non-existent or inappropriate an alternative system of evaluation is required. The prices determined under this system are referred to as *shadow prices* or *administrative prices*. Shadow prices are 'invented' or 'made up' by the analyst to reflect the value of the costs and benefits concerned as accurately as possible. For example, a typical shadow price would be the hourly wage rate to be used in evaluating the time saved by motorists able to use a new road.

More difficult problems arise if a project will result in an increase or a decrease in the incidence of death (eg if a motorway is built the number of road deaths may alter). CBA requires that a monetary value be placed on this change in mortality rates in order to assess the 'cost' or 'benefit' to society. There are obviously immense problems in putting a monetary value on human life. From society's point of view an individual life will rarely be totally worthless, nor will it be infinitely valuable. Any method of valuing a life must be fallible. For example, if a value was derived by considering the expected future contribution to production over the human's lifetime then this would suggest

Investment appraisal

that the life of a pensioner or a disabled person would have a negative value.

One method of measuring the value of externalities is to ask those who benefit (suffer) from them how much they would be prepared to pay in order to prevent (ensure) the removal of those externalities. The problem of this 'willingness to pay' approach lies in eliciting honest responses to the question.

The effect of some externalities which affect all members of a given geographical area may be reflected in the change in the market prices of houses in that area as a result of the appearance of the externality. This indicates the monetary value (whether positive or negative) placed on the externality by householders in that area.

Inevitably there will always be difficulties in assigning monetary values to many of the costs and benefits which arise out of a capital project. However, we cannot exclude these costs and benefits from our analysis simply because there are measurement problems.

Shadow prices are necessary if the costs and benefits are to be evaluated in terms which are equivalent to expenditures and receipts in the private sector. They are, however, liable to considerable bias, especially if they are being used to evaluate new types of spending. Because of this particular problem it is often thought that CBA is best used when comparing projects of a similar nature (eg in choosing between alternative road improvement schemes) rather than to compare projects which are completely different in nature (eg reservoirs and school expansion programmes). This problem becomes especially acute when an attempt is made to compare public expenditure to private expenditure, whose value *can* be clearly established in financial terms. The problems outlined above do not render cost-benefit analysis useless in the choice between alternative, dissimilar projects – they do, however, demonstrate some of the limitations of the technique and encourage care in the interpretation of the results of any study.

3. Investment Method

Having established which costs and benefits to include in the analysis, and having valued them in money terms, the next step is to consider the timing of the flows and costs of benefits. This is important because costs or benefits encountered in the future are worth less in present values. The flows of costs and benefits should then be evaluated for each year of the project so that either the *net present value* or the *yield* can be calculated. When this is established the project can be compared with the returns on alternative projects to see whether it is worthwhile in terms of the efficient use of scarce resources.

The Choice of the Discount Rate

For a project to be considered worthwhile it must show a return at least as great as the alternative projects which must be given up – ie there is an *opportunity cost* facing each project in terms of the alternative foregone; the project under consideration can be thought worthwhile only if it is better than these alternatives.

The *net present value* method of appraisal requires the use of the opportunity cost rate of discount in the discounting procedure. If the NPV of the project exceeds zero then the project is worthwhile. Alternatively, the *yield method* requires that the yields on alternative projects are known so that comparisons can be made. If the yield of the project under consideration exceeds that of the alternatives then the project is worthwhile.

Both the NPV and the yield method therefore require a measure of the opportunity cost of the capital employed. Once this is established it can be used as the discount rate. The establishment of this rate of interest does however lead to difficulties for there are innumerable degrees of risk, knowledge, liquidity etc. Ideally the rate chosen should be that of marginal risk-free projects of similar project life, and the problem of risk should be treated separately. Two possible practical solutions suggest themselves:

1. The project should be discounted at a number of different discount rates and only if it appears worthwhile under most circumstances should it be accepted – a very cautious approach.

2. The long-term cost of borrowing to the government on its bonds could be used as an indication of the risk-free rate. Unfortunately different government bonds offer different

Investment appraisal

yields, so it may be unclear which is the most appropriate rate to use.

The Treatment of Distributional Effects

Cost-benefit analysis considers only the relationship between gains and losses from a project and ignores the problem of who gains and who loses. This ought to be taken into account under certain circumstances:

1. Where the losses of some groups are very high and no compensation is to be paid, eg environmental damage to a town sited close to a new or expanded airport.

2. Where redistributional objectives are part of the public sector's spending policies, eg urban renewal schemes aimed at improving the housing situation for people in relatively low income groups. In the event of redistributional effects being important, then the gains registered from an economic point of view should be considered in the light of whether the income distribution effects are deemed to be satisfactory. It might be considered, for example, that a project with a high yield but regressive income distribution effects should be scrapped, whereas a project with a low yield but favourable income distribution effects should be accepted.

Conclusions

1. CBA aims at helping public sector decision-makers in their choice of projects, particularly those such as urban renewal, roads, reservoirs and education, where the costs and benefits are general, non-financial and extend over a long period of time.

2. Efficiency in public sector decision-making is achieved by establishing the returns from public projects in terms which are comparable with each other *and* within the private sector. CBA helps to establish whether scarce resources will be used more *effectively* within the public sector.

3. There are many diffiiculties involved in the establishment of

cost-benefit data, particularly the risk of bias on the part of the analyst. Care must therefore be taken in interpreting results.

4. CBA is a criterion of *economic efficiency* but this criterion is not necessarily the best as it may conflict with other, possibly superior, criteria such as the democratic voting process. It is a tool for aiding public decision-making to achieve *consistent, economic solutions* by channeling resources into those projects which will offer the greatest increase in the net benefit enjoyed by society.

Examples

(a) Motorway Scheme

COSTS	BENEFITS
Capital costs of construction	Reduced time for journeys
Land costs	Reduced congestion on alternative routes
Environmental damage	Reduction in accidents
	Reduced wear and tear on vehicles

(b) Urban Renewal

COSTS	BENEFITS
Loss of old buildings	Value of new buildings
Capital costs of new buildings	Enhanced value of buildings and environment in surrounding area

Investment appraisal

(c) Reservoir Scheme

COSTS	BENEFITS
Loss of agricultural land, houses, farms etc.	Improved water supply
Environmental damage (eg visual)	Gains from flood control
Ecological damage	Better recreational facilities (eg sailing)

9.
Control of the Investment Process

Throughout this work, a number of tacit assumptions have been made. These have enabled us to explain investment appraisal free from the everyday distractions of the outside world. These assumptions largely hinge upon the human element, for human beings act from a number of motives, which may not always be rational in an economic sense, and which complicate the task of appraising investment options. The most important of these assumptions can be highlighted:

1. Only quantifiable consequences of investment matter, ie investments are not judged on any moral, aesthetic or political criteria.

2. Investment options simply emerge. No long process (which itself costs money) is needed in order to identify profitable investments.

3. Estimates of future cash flows are free from bias. 'Pet' projects (ie those with particular appeal to the decision-maker, for whatever personal reason) are not promoted through deliberate underestimation of their costs and overestimation of their returns.

4. Risk can be allowed for by using adjustments to the net present value analysis.

These assumptions are of course unrealistic; the world simply does not function in this way. It is for these sorts of reasons that the investment process is controlled, both by means of a corporate structure established to authorise the implementation of investments, and by a system designed to monitor investments for the benefit of particular projects and to

Investment appraisal

help improve the whole process of investment selection and implementation.

The company must decide on a structure for investment decision-making. It must decide how far the investment process should be decentralised and delegated. All investment proposals might be given to an investment manager and he may in turn delegate investments below a certain capital requirement or below a certain level of risk, or up to a given level of strategic importance. It may be noted that such a policy fits in well with a policy of 'management by exception' which only brings affairs to the notice of management when significant deviations from the plans occur. The essence of this concept is, 'when business is functioning smoothly, leave well alone'.

Project Authorisation

In practice, once an investment proposal has been evaluated and once it has reached the top rung of the authorisation ladder, it is usually implemented. This is mainly because a great deal of effort and resources have been used to get it so far. Also, the project is likely to be a sound and meritorious option simply by virtue of the fact that it has advanced so far through the appraisal process. Buiding up support from its own internal dynamics, complete rejection of a project is rare, though it may be returned for further consideration. Often, it is the case that the reputation of the proposer of the investment is as important as the relative merits of the investment itself. A manager with a proven track record of putting forward profitable investments will stand a much better chance of having a proposal accepted than a colleague with a more chequered career, irrespective of the relative financial merits of the particular investments in question. It may also be the case that at this stage the decision will be taken to undertake a marginal project rather than reject it since the planning costs and certain capital costs have already been incurred.

Project Control and Post-audits

Project control is concerned simply with the monitoring of the project throughout its life. The most important tool of project control is the post-audit. The ICMA in 1984 defined the post-audit as,

Project control and post-audits

'an objective and independent appraisal of the measure of success of a capital expenditure project in progressing the business as planned. The appraisal should cover the implementation of the project from authorisation to commissioning and its technical and commercial performance after commissioning.'

Thus, the post-audit will be concerned with how the project is progressing in reality, and how this reality differs from the forecasts on which its acceptance was based. The post-audit will look at the assumptions on which the investment was estimated as being profitable. If, for example, the investment was based on an assumption that the market would grow at a rate of 5% per annum and that its market share would remain constant at 20%, the post-audit will need to know if the market expansion is growing at that rate and if increased competition (or its reverse) is going to lead to a change in market share. The post-audit will also look at the actual cash flow figures and compare them with the estimated cash flows. Variance analysis would be of help here. Using modern computers, differences in actual and expected costs and earnings can be brought to the attention of the investigators, again facilitating the use of management by exception.

Post-audits can be said to have two main purposes. The first purpose is to provide a basis for remedial action if the investment is not proceeding according to plan. If the project cash flows are worse than expected, then the post-audit should identify the reason for this and be a basis for deciding whether the investment can and should be scaled down, whether a second phase should be delayed or, at worst, whether the investment should be abandoned. On the reverse side, of course, better than expected cash flows might lead to an expansion of the investment or other possible options.

The second purpose, and benefit, of the post-audit is to improve the general quality of decision-making. Those managers responsible for planning investments will be made more accountable for their actions. The lack of a post-audit can be said to encourage overly optimistic estimates of the profitability of an investment. At the very least, they are not discouraged. The knowledge that the accuracy of cash flow estimates will be under examination during the post-audit will encourage managers to be strictly objective in their estimates of the viability of investment

Investment appraisal

options. Pet projects are less likely to be pushed. The post-audit must not tend to encourage undue conservatism, however. This would lead to managers pursuing a satisficing policy towards profits, following the motto 'anything for a quiet life'. The post-audit should also be of use in helping to avoid repeating mistakes made in the past. Where the post-audit discovers an investment going awry it has a diagnostic role of discovering what went wrong, where, when and why. Such knowledge may be invaluable when it comes to deciding on a similar investment option in the future.

Post-audit Planning

Post-audits are no panacea for all investment ills, however. This is because, in the first case, no panacea can ever exist and, more helpfully, because post-audits can be expensive and time-consuming. Post-audits rightly, therefore, tend to concentrate on the biggest and most important investments. Any other policy would simply not be cost-effective.

For this same reason of cost-effectiveness, post-audits should concentrate on those assumptions and variables which have the greatest impact on the investment project and which may be critical to the success or failure of the project. Sensitivity analysis will be of help in identifying these critical areas. The timing of the post-audit may itself be affected by such factors (when they are obvious). Where an investment, for example, depends for its success on the setting up of a distribution chain for a project, it will make sense for the post-audit to be carried out soon after this process has been scheduled to finish.

The post-audit should report fully on all aspects of the investment, and it is not only the complex financial details that are important – so-called non-economic aspects have to be included. These may include the impact that the investment will have with regard to the corporate image of the firm, to the environment and on the morale of the workforce. This is because these factors may well have long-term costs (both tangible and intangible). The result of a dissatisfied labour force may be a strike which very definitely does have a financial cost.

Finally, it should be stressed that the assessment of the investment in the post-audit should be made in terms of its original purpose. If the overriding aim of the project is to dominate a market which is expected to grow in the longer term, then a post-audit which criticises the investment after two years for poor profitability has manifestly missed the point. Properly conducted, however, and with a wide ranging but relevant brief, the post-audit should be of great benefit to the firm and its investment decision-making process.

10.
Theory and Practice

As one might expect, the theory and practice of investment appraisal vary considerably. This work has been unashamedly directed towards the theoretical side of investment appraisal because relevant theory is an invaluable aid to the success of any investment venture. This is not to say, of course, that theory is always superior to practice; that where theory and practice are in conflict, practice is in error and should fall into line with what theory dictates. Rather, practice should be based upon theory; but the manager does not need to be told that if an investment is a failure, it is his head which is on the line and not the theory maker's.

It is of interest to see to what extent the theory which has been outlined in this book is used by industry to solve its everyday investment problems. Where theory and practice are in conflict, it will be the aim to understand why this is, rather than to castigate industry for not following the help and advice which works of this sort give.

It should be pointed out here that the academic research and surveys on which this chapter is based have been concerned almost exclusively with the very largest companies in the UK, in paricular, and also in the US. It is safe to assume that any conclusions that can be reached as to trends concerning the use of theory in companies according to their size will hold good as we go down the scale of industry. Indeed, if anything, these trends are likely to become even more marked.

Let us look, therefore, at how companies arrive at their investment decisions, paying particular attention to how the methods of investment appraisal we have discussed are used in practice.

Payback

Payback is undoubtedly the most popular method of analysis in practice, and this is as true for the larger firms as for the small. Pike, in *Capital Budgeting* in the 1980s (ICMA 1982) found that 79% of the firms surveyed (and they were 150 of the largest firms in the UK) used payback as a means of investment appraisal. The fact that only 32% of firms used payback as a primay evaluation method and that 90% of firms which used more than one method of analysis used payback as one of those methods, strongly suggests that payback is often seen as a back-up method for more sophisticated and theoretically superior techniques. This back-up valve is enhanced by the fact that payback is a method whose whole purpose is often quoted (rightly or wrongly) as being to ensure against the presence of risk in an undertaking. Analysed industry by industry, payback is almost universally popular – 84% of capital goods firms and 94.1% of consumer durables firms use payback as an evaluation technique. That only 55% of storage firms use payback is not so much evidence of investment sophistication as a pointer to the fact that investments are less critical in this type of industry.

The popularity of the payback technique is due mostly to the fact that it is easy to understand and simple to use. Its theoretical drawbacks were pointed out by most of the respondents who did not use the technique. That they are in the minority must be stressed, and typifying those who use the technqiue was the comment,

> 'It is simple, quick to produce and readily understood particulaly by non-financial overextended management.'

Accounting Rate of Return

This was a less popular form of analysis than payback but 51% of firms in the Pike survey did use this technique. Accounting rate of return is an attempt to meaure profitability, but in doing so it lends itself to criticism because it disregards the time value of money. Its popularity is due to the fact that it relates the return on an investment to the business as a whole. Analysing by industry, ARR is most popular with capital goods firms, 67% of those surveyed use it, as do 55% of storage firms. The chemical and oil industries, which tend towards more sophistication,

Investment appraisal

use it much less, with only 26% of respondents admitting to its use.

Discounting Methods

As we have seen, the methods of discounting are NPV (which gives a positive or negative value to future cash flows discounted so as to give a present value) and IRR (which is the percentage discount rate which needs to be applied to give an NPV of zero). For a variety of reasons, we concluded that NPV was superior to IRR and demonstrated this with the aid of examples. It is therefore interesting, not to say disconcerting, to find that IRR is by a comfortable margin the more popular technique, with 54% of respondents using IRR and only 28% using NPV. Furthermore 41% of firms used IRR as a primary evaluation method whereas only 17% used NPV in this way. It is here that the size of the concern is important in determining whether these more elaborate techniques are used. Whereas 30% of firms with a capital budget below £5,000,000 used NPV, 61% of firms with a capital budget in excesss of £50,000,000 used NPV. This trend is even more marked with IRR. It might be tempting to conclude that the larger firms understand better the theory and implication of discounted cash-flow analysis and, while this is true to some extent, it fails to explain why IRR is used in preference to NPV. Those companies which used NPV tended to cite as justification the theoretical and thus, in the final analysis, practical advantages of NPV, pointing out the problems associated with IRR conditions of non-conventional cash-flows. IRR was more popular essentially because its characteristic of using a percentage rate makes it easy to understand and be explained to those managers without theoretical financial knowledge. IRR was also preferred because respondents believed IRR to be a superior method of ranking alternatives. This led Pike to conclude that,

> 'The question of which discounting method is best suited for ranking projects has been much discussed in the literature but would appear to be foreign to most managers.'

This type of conclusion is similar to that of Scapens, Sale and Tikkas in *The Financial Control of Divisional Capital Investment*

(ICMA 1982) who concluded that,

> 'The picture to emerge . . . is not one of rigorous financial analysis of the capital investment proposals.'

The UK seems to lag behind US industry in the sophistication of investment appraisal. Thus, Scapens, Sale and Tikkas find that whereas only 54% of top British firms use some form of DCF analysis, the comparable figure for the US is 84%. The use of DCF is increasing in Britain, however. Britain saw IRR analysis increase in popularity (according to Pike) from 42% to 54% beteen 1975 and 1980, and NPV increase from 32% to 38% during the same years. Thus the trend is undoubtedly towards greater sophistication as managers become increasingly *au fait* with the theory of investment appraisal.

Risk-appraisal Techniques

Surveys have repeatedly shown that a clear majority of firms do not formally analyse risk. Pike found that only 37% of the firms sampled analyse risk. When it is remembered that his sample was 150 firms within the bracket of the 300 largest quoted companies, it can be appreciated that for the majority of businesses, risk is hardly assessed, if at all. Of the methods of risk analysis, sensitivity analysis was bound to be the most popular, and this popularity increased as the size of the capital budget increased. Shortening the payback period was also another popular method of dealing with risk, and was of increased importance as the size of capital budgets was reduced. Risk appraisal too seems to be increasing in popularity over time. For example, only 24% of the firms used sensitivity analysis in 1975, but by 1980–81 that figure had increased to 38%. Despite this increased use of risk analysis, it does seem that the most notable point is that so few of even the largest companies use it. The reasons for this seem to be that the necessary analysis is both complex and time-consuming and that risk is itself impossible to quantify and therefore of negligible practical benefit. Even some firms who did use risk analysis did so with caution, if not with distrust. Other firms however were enthusiastic about its benefits. Sensitivity analysis was singled out for mention as being useful because it gave information as to which were the key

Investment appraisal

variables to be assessed and monitored once the investment was in operation. So, the trend is for increased use of some sort of risk analysis, though inbuilt resistance to such methods may stop it gaining similar acceptance to discounted cash flow methods of investment appraisal.

Post-audits

Both Scapens, Sale and Tikkas and Pike found that a majority of firms surveyed did not use post-completion audits. Pike's survey found that only 36% did so, whereas Scapens *et al* found a higher figure, 48%. Both studies found that the incidence of post-audits increased according to the scale of the enterprise involved. Moreover, their use has increased over time, Scapens *et al* finding a 1975–80 increase of 16 percentage points from 32% to 48%; for the purpose of comparison between firms, it should be pointed out that post-audits seem to vary in scope, size and timing. It seems that post-audits are used mainly because of their contribution to learning processes as far as investment in practice is concerned. Most firms appear to find that audits are generally completed too late to have any bearing on whether an investment can be modified so as to make it successful if it is failing. This learning from past mistakes is allied to the fact that post-audits make managers more accountable and therefore responsible. As one company accountant quoted in Scapens *et al* commented:

> 'Since introducing post-completion audits we have found a substantial improvement in project proposals . . . the effect of post-completion audits is mainly psychological.'

It must be said that even though those firms which conduct post-audits are pleased with the resulting benefits, the majority of firms did not bother to conduct them. The reasons for this are that many firms think post-audits are a waste of time if a position cannot be rectified, that they are not cost-effective and that if adequate controls are put on at the spending stage, the post-audit is unnecessary.

That the use of post-audits is the norm rather than the exception in America, and that they are becoming even more common in the UK, suggests that their benefits are becoming more clearly recognised.

Conclusion

It is apparent that a considerable, though closing, gap between theory and practice does exist. It is not credible to explain this away by saying that industry is run by managers who are obtuse and benighted. Neither is it the case that academics are aloof inhabitants of ivory towers churning out abstruse theory. Rather, it should be explained in terms of an inbuilt resistance to change; of managers favouring the practical and maintaining a healthy scepticism towards theory until it can be shown to work for them. Even having said that, it would be myopic not to see that the explanation is still far from complete. Over time, however, methods of investment appraisal are changing and practice is falling more into line with theory, though how far and how quickly is still unclear. Up-to-date studies would help show the changing face of industry and investment practices within it. There is a need for these, and also for closer looks at how the smaller businesses, as opposed to the giants which are at the centre of most studies, conduct their investment appraisal. What does seem clear is that there is still room for a more theoretical approach to investment appraisal within commerce and industry.

Appendix I
Present Value Tables

Table A
PRESENT VALUE OF £1

Years Hence	1%	2%	4%	6%	8%	10%	12%	14%	15%	16%	18%	20%	22%	24%	25%	26%	28%	30%	35%	40%	45%	50%
1	0.990	0.980	0.962	0.943	0.926	0.909	0.893	0.877	0.870	0.862	0.847	0.833	0.820	0.806	0.800	0.794	0.781	0.769	0.741	0.714	0.690	0.667
2	0.980	0.961	0.925	0.890	0.857	0.826	0.797	0.769	0.756	0.743	0.718	0.694	0.672	0.650	0.640	0.630	0.610	0.592	0.549	0.510	0.476	0.444
3	0.971	0.942	0.889	0.840	0.794	0.751	0.712	0.675	0.658	0.641	0.609	0.579	0.551	0.524	0.512	0.500	0.477	0.455	0.406	0.364	0.328	0.296
4	0.961	0.924	0.855	0.792	0.735	0.683	0.636	0.592	0.572	0.552	0.516	0.482	0.451	0.423	0.410	0.397	0.373	0.350	0.301	0.260	0.226	0.198
5	0.951	0.906	0.822	0.747	0.681	0.621	0.567	0.519	0.497	0.476	0.437	0.402	0.370	0.341	0.328	0.315	0.291	0.269	0.223	0.186	0.156	0.132
6	0.942	0.888	0.790	0.705	0.630	0.564	0.507	0.456	0.432	0.410	0.370	0.335	0.303	0.275	0.262	0.250	0.227	0.207	0.165	0.133	0.108	0.088
7	0.933	0.871	0.760	0.665	0.583	0.513	0.452	0.400	0.376	0.354	0.314	0.279	0.249	0.222	0.210	0.198	0.178	0.159	0.122	0.095	0.074	0.059
8	0.923	0.853	0.731	0.627	0.540	0.467	0.404	0.351	0.327	0.305	0.266	0.233	0.204	0.179	0.168	0.157	0.139	0.123	0.091	0.068	0.051	0.039
9	0.914	0.837	0.703	0.592	0.500	0.424	0.361	0.308	0.284	0.263	0.225	0.194	0.167	0.144	0.134	0.125	0.108	0.094	0.067	0.048	0.035	0.026
10	0.905	0.820	0.676	0.558	0.463	0.386	0.322	0.270	0.247	0.227	0.191	0.162	0.137	0.116	0.107	0.099	0.085	0.073	0.050	0.035	0.024	0.017
11	0.896	0.804	0.650	0.527	0.429	0.350	0.287	0.237	0.215	0.195	0.162	0.135	0.112	0.094	0.086	0.079	0.066	0.056	0.037	0.025	0.017	0.012
12	0.887	0.788	0.625	0.497	0.397	0.319	0.257	0.208	0.187	0.168	0.137	0.112	0.092	0.076	0.069	0.062	0.052	0.043	0.027	0.018	0.012	0.008
13	0.879	0.773	0.601	0.469	0.368	0.290	0.229	0.182	0.163	0.145	0.116	0.093	0.075	0.061	0.055	0.050	0.040	0.033	0.020	0.013	0.008	0.005
14	0.870	0.758	0.577	0.442	0.340	0.263	0.205	0.160	0.141	0.125	0.099	0.078	0.062	0.049	0.044	0.039	0.032	0.025	0.015	0.009	0.006	0.003
15	0.861	0.743	0.555	0.417	0.315	0.239	0.183	0.140	0.123	0.108	0.084	0.065	0.051	0.040	0.035	0.031	0.025	0.020	0.011	0.006	0.004	0.002
16	0.853	0.728	0.534	0.394	0.292	0.218	0.163	0.123	0.107	0.093	0.071	0.054	0.042	0.032	0.028	0.025	0.019	0.015	0.008	0.005	0.003	0.002
17	0.844	0.714	0.513	0.371	0.270	0.198	0.146	0.108	0.093	0.080	0.060	0.045	0.034	0.026	0.023	0.020	0.015	0.012	0.006	0.003	0.002	0.001
18	0.836	0.700	0.494	0.350	0.250	0.180	0.130	0.095	0.081	0.069	0.051	0.038	0.028	0.021	0.018	0.016	0.012	0.009	0.005	0.003	0.001	0.001
19	0.828	0.686	0.475	0.331	0.232	0.164	0.116	0.083	0.070	0.060	0.043	0.031	0.023	0.017	0.014	0.012	0.009	0.007	0.003	0.002	0.001	
20	0.820	0.673	0.456	0.312	0.215	0.149	0.104	0.073	0.061	0.051	0.037	0.026	0.019	0.014	0.012	0.010	0.007	0.005	0.002	0.001		
21	0.811	0.660	0.439	0.294	0.199	0.135	0.093	0.064	0.053	0.044	0.031	0.022	0.015	0.011	0.009	0.008	0.006	0.004	0.002	0.001		
22	0.803	0.647	0.422	0.278	0.184	0.123	0.083	0.056	0.046	0.038	0.026	0.018	0.013	0.009	0.007	0.006	0.004	0.003	0.001	0.001		
23	0.795	0.634	0.406	0.262	0.170	0.112	0.074	0.049	3.040	0.033	0.022	0.015	0.010	0.007	0.006	0.005	0.003	0.002	0.001			
24	0.788	0.622	0.390	0.247	0.158	0.102	0.066	0.043	0.035	0.028	0.019	0.013	0.008	0.006	0.005	0.004	0.003	0.002	0.001			
25	0.780	0.610	0.375	0.233	0.146	0.092	0.059	0.038	0.030	0.024	0.016	0.010	0.007	0.005	0.004	0.003	0.002	0.001	0.001			
26	0.772	0.598	0.361	0.220	0.135	0.084	0.053	0.033	0.026	0.021	0.014	0.009	0.006	0.004	0.003	0.002	0.002	0.001				
27	0.764	0.586	0.347	0.207	0.125	0.076	0.047	0.029	0.023	0.018	0.011	0.007	0.005	0.003	0.002	0.002	0.001	0.001				
28	0.757	0.574	0.333	0.196	0.116	0.069	0.042	0.026	0.020	0.016	0.010	0.006	0.004	0.002	0.002	0.002	0.001	0.001				
29	0.749	0.563	0.321	0.185	0.107	0.063	0.037	0.022	0.017	0.014	0.008	0.005	0.003	0.002	0.002	0.001	0.001					
30	0.742	0.552	0.308	0.174	0.099	0.057	0.033	0.020	0.015	0.012	0.007	0.004	0.003	0.002	0.001	0.001						
40	0.672	0.453	0.208	0.097	0.046	0.022	0.011	0.005	0.004	0.003	0.001	0.001										
50	0.608	0.372	0.141	0.054	0.021	0.009	0.003	0.001	0.001	0.001												

Table B

PRESENT VALUE OF £1 RECEIVED ANNUALLY FOR N YEARS

Years (N)	1%	2%	4%	6%	8%	10%	12%	14%	15%	16%	18%	20%	22%	24%	25%	26%	28%	30%	35%	40%	45%	50%
1	0.990	0.980	0.962	0.943	0.926	0.909	0.893	0.877	0.670	0.862	0.847	0.833	0.820	0.806	0.800	0.794	0.781	0.769	0.741	0.714	0.690	0.667
2	1.970	1.942	1.886	1.833	1.783	1.736	1.690	1.647	1.626	1.605	1.566	1.528	1.492	1.457	1.440	1.424	1.392	1.361	1.289	1.224	1.165	1.111
3	2.941	2.884	2.775	2.673	2.577	2.487	2.402	2.322	2.283	2.246	2.174	2.106	2.042	1.981	1.952	1.923	1.868	1.816	1.696	1.589	1.493	1.407
4	3.902	3.808	3.630	3.465	3.312	3.170	3.037	2.914	2.855	2.798	2.690	2.589	2.494	2.404	2.362	2.320	2.241	2.166	1.997	1.849	1.720	1.605
5	4.853	4.713	4.452	4.212	3.993	3.791	3.605	3.433	3.352	3.274	3.127	2.991	2.864	2.745	2.689	2.635	2.532	2.436	2.220	2.035	1.876	1.737
6	5.795	5.601	5.242	4.917	4.623	4.355	4.111	3.889	3.784	3.685	3.498	3.326	3.167	3.020	2.951	2.885	2.759	2.643	2.385	2.168	1.983	1.824
7	6.728	6.472	6.002	5.582	5.206	4.868	4.564	4.288	4.160	4.039	3.812	3.605	3.416	3.242	3.161	3.083	2.937	2.802	2.508	2.263	2.057	1.883
8	7.652	7.325	6.733	6.210	5.747	5.335	4.968	4.639	4.487	4.344	4.078	3.837	3.619	3.421	3.329	3.241	3.076	2.925	2.598	2.331	2.108	1.922
9	8.566	8.162	7.435	6.802	6.247	5.759	5.328	4.946	4.772	4.607	4.303	4.031	3.786	3.566	3.463	3.366	3.184	3.019	2.665	2.379	2.144	1.948
10	9.471	8.983	8.111	7.360	6.710	6.145	5.650	5.216	5.019	4.833	4.494	4.192	3.923	3.682	3.571	3.465	3.269	3.092	2.715	2.414	2.168	1.965
11	10.368	9.787	8.760	7.887	7.139	6.495	5.937	5.453	5.234	5.029	4.656	4.327	4.035	3.776	3.656	3.544	3.335	3.147	2.752	2.438	2.185	1.977
12	11.255	10.575	9.385	8.384	7.536	6.814	6.194	5.660	5.421	5.197	4.793	4.439	4.127	3.851	3.725	3.606	3.387	3.190	2.779	2.456	2.196	1.985
13	12.134	11.343	9.986	8.853	7.904	7.103	6.424	5.842	5.583	5.342	4.910	4.533	4.203	3.912	3.780	3.656	3.427	3.223	2.799	2.468	2.204	1.990
14	13.004	12.106	10.563	9.295	8.244	7.367	6.628	6.002	5.724	5.468	5.008	4.611	4.265	3.962	3.824	3.695	3.459	3.249	2.814	2.477	2.210	1.993
15	13.865	12.849	11.118	9.712	8.559	7.606	6.811	6.142	5.847	5.575	5.092	4.675	4.315	4.001	3.859	3.726	3.483	3.268	2.825	2.484	2.214	1.995
16	14.718	13.578	11.652	10.106	8.851	7.824	6.974	6.265	5.954	5.669	5.162	4.730	4.357	4.033	3.887	3.751	3.503	3.283	2.834	2.489	2.216	1.997
17	15.562	14.292	12.166	10.477	9.122	8.022	7.120	6.373	6.047	5.749	5.222	4.775	4.391	4.059	3.910	3.771	3.518	3.295	2.840	2.492	2.218	1.998
18	16.398	14.992	12.659	10.828	9.372	8.201	7.250	6.467	6.128	5.818	5.273	4.812	4.419	4.080	3.928	3.786	3.529	3.304	2.844	2.494	2.219	1.999
19	17.226	15.678	13.134	11.158	9.604	8.365	7.366	6.550	6.198	5.877	5.316	4.844	4.442	4.097	3.942	3.799	3.539	3.311	2.848	2.496	2.220	1.999
20	18.046	16.351	13.590	11.470	9.818	8.514	7.469	6.623	6.259	5.929	5.353	4.870	4.460	4.110	3.954	3.808	3.546	3.316	2.850	2.497	2.221	1.999
21	18.857	17.011	14.029	11.764	10.017	8.649	7.562	6.687	6.312	5.973	5.384	4.891	4.476	4.121	3.963	3.816	3.551	3.320	2.852	2.498	2.221	2.000
22	19.660	17.658	14.451	12.042	10.201	8.772	7.645	6.743	6.359	6.011	5.410	4.909	4.488	4.130	3.970	3.822	3.556	3.323	2.853	2.498	2.222	2.000
23	20.456	18.292	14.857	12.303	10.371	8.883	7.718	6.792	6.399	6.044	5.432	4.925	4.499	4.137	3.976	3.827	3.559	3.325	2.854	2.499	2.222	2.000
24	21.243	18.914	15.247	12.550	10.529	8.985	7.784	6.835	6.434	6.073	5.451	4.937	4.507	4.143	3.981	3.831	3.562	3.327	2.855	2.499	2.222	2.000
25	22.023	19.523	15.622	12.783	10.675	9.077	7.843	6.873	6.464	6.097	5.467	4.948	4.514	4.147	3.985	3.834	3.564	3.329	2.856	2.499	2.222	2.000
26	22.795	20.121	15.983	13.003	10.810	9.161	7.896	6.906	6.491	6.118	5.480	4.956	4.520	4.151	3.988	3.837	3.566	3.330	2.856	2.500	2.222	2.000
27	23.560	20.707	16.330	13.211	10.935	9.237	7.943	6.935	6.514	6.136	5.492	4.964	4.524	4.154	3.990	3.839	3.567	3.331	2.856	2.500	2.222	2.000
28	24.316	21.281	16.663	13.406	11.051	9.307	7.984	6.961	6.534	6.152	5.502	4.970	4.528	4.157	3.992	3.840	3.568	3.331	2.857	2.500	2.222	2.000
29	25.066	21.844	16.984	13.591	11.158	9.370	8.022	6.983	6.551	6.166	5.510	4.975	4.531	4.159	3.994	3.841	3.569	3.332	2.857	2.500	2.222	2.000
30	25.808	22.396	17.292	13.765	11.258	9.427	8.055	7.003	6.566	6.177	5.517	4.979	4.534	4.160	3.995	3.842	3.569	3.332	2.857	2.500	2.222	2.000
40	32.835	27.355	19.793	15.046	11.925	9.779	8.244	7.105	6.642	6.234	5.548	4.997	4.544	4.166	3.999	3.846	3.571	3.333	2.857	2.500	2.222	2.000
50	39.196	31.424	21.482	15.762	12.234	9.915	8.304	7.133	6.661	6.246	5.554	4.999	4.545	4.167	4.000	3.846	3.571	3.333	2.857	2.500	2.222	2.000

From Management Accounting, Text and Cases. By R. N. Anthony.
Richard D. Irwin, Inc. 94/- (£4.70).

Index

accounting rate of return, 133-4
    return on investment, 13, 23-5
administrative prices, 121
annual equivalent annuity, 110-14
assets
    capital allowances, 104-6
    replacement decisions, 106-16

bad debts, 104
balancing charge, 106
bank loan (cost), 58-9
basket of goods, 100
Bayes-Laplace criterion, 66-7
benefit cost ratios, 89-92, 93
beta factor (investment), 78-9
borrowing, 43, 102-3
    cost of, *see* capital, cost of
break-even analysis, 80
Bromwich, 11
Buchanan Report, 121
buy/lease decisions, 114-16

capital
    allowances, 104-6
    asset pricing model, 50, 75-6
    costs (of assets), 107
    markets, 14-19, 33
    mix, 56, 59-60
    outlay (initial), 38-9
Capital Budgeting, 133
capital, cost of, 107
    capital structure, 45, 59-63
    each type of finance, 48-54

equity, 47-8
    weighted average, 29, 54-9, 61-3, 75-6
capital rationing, 88
    hard and soft, 88-9
    multi-period, 40, 92-7
    single period, 35-6, 89-92
capital structure, 45
    Modigliani-Miller approach, 59, 61-3
    traditionalist approach, 59, 60-61
cash flow
    discounted, *see* discounted cash flow
    incremental, 36-7, 38
Central Statistical Office, 104
certainty, 94, 97
Chartism, 18
compounding, 27, 28
computer simulation, 81
constant returns to scale, 94, 97
constraint expressions, 94-5, 96
corporation tax, 56, 103-6
cost-benefit analysis, 117-19
    discount rate, 123-4
    distributional effects, 124
    examples, 125-6
    stages, 120-23
cost of capital, *see* capital, cost of
cost of finance, 48-54
critical variables, 79-80

Index

death, monetary value of, 121-2
debt capital (cost), 50-52, 58
   effect of taxation, 53-4
decision-making
   introduction to, 11-19
   risk, 11, 13, 71-9
   uncertainty, 13, 14, 64-71
decision tree analysis, 13, 83-7
dependent projects, 40-41
depreciation, 23-4, 104
Descarte's rule, 34
discounted cash flows
   internal rate of return, 14, 28, 30-34, 36-41, 42-4, 134, 135
   net present value, 13, 14, 28-36, 38-44, 134-5
   time value of money, 21-2, 26-8
discounting, 27, 28, 29-31
   methods, 134-5
distributional effects, 124
diversification, 77-8, 84
dividend growth model, 48, 49
divisibility, 94, 97
double-counting, 120
'downside risk', 67, 68

economic efficiency, 125
efficiency (public sector), 124, 125
efficient market hypothesis, 17-19
entertainment expenses, 104
equity, 47
   cost of, 48-50, 58
excess returns, 18, 19
exchange rates, 13
expected values for NPV, 82-3, 86-7
expenses (disallowed), 103-4
external capital rationing, 88-9
externalities, 118-19, 121, 122

factory size, 65-70
Financial Control of Capital
Investment, 14
financial leases, 114
Financial Times all share index, 78
Firth, 11
'fishbait' method, 21
'Fisher' rate, 36, 38
freerider, 118
fundamental analysis, 18

game theory, 65-71
gearing, 45, 60
   WACC and, 61-3
Gordon's model, 48
government bonds, 123-4

hard rationing, 88-9
Hurwicz criterion, 68-9

ICMA, 14, 128, 133
imperfect capital market, 16-17
incremental cash flow, 36-7, 38
independent projects, 33
inflation, 26, 46-7, 98-103, 107
information (perfect/complete), 12
   efficient market hypothesis, 17-19
Inland Revenue, 103, 104, 106
'inside' information, 18-19
insignificant effects, 120
intangibles, 121
integer programming, 97
interest rate
   capital markets and, 15-16
   cost of capital and, 46-7, 50, 51, 53-5
   real, 99, 100
   time value of money, 26, 27-8
intermediaries, 15
internal rate of return, 14, 28, 36-41, 135
   calculation of, 30-34
   merits, 42

Index

    multiple, 41, 43
    NPV and (comparison), 42-4, 134
interpolation method, 31-2, 52
investment
    incentives, 107
    options, 15-16, 17-19, 33
    process (control), 127-31
    scale of (differences), 36-9
    strategy, 93-7
investment appraisal
    applications of, 98-116
    decisions, *see* decision-making
    public sector, 117-26
    theory and practice, 132-6
    traditional approaches, 20-25
    WACC (use of), 56-9
Investment Appraisal, 30, 77, 89
irredeemable debentures, 50-51
Issues in Finance, 11

Keane, Simon, 11, 40
knowledge (of options), 12, 13

lease/buy decisions, 114-16
linear programming, 93-7
liquidation, 54
loans, 14-19, 33, 58-9
Lower, J.F., 116
lowest common multiple method, 107-10
Lumby, 30, 77, 89

maintenance costs, 107-9, 110-16
managers, 128, 137
    accountability, 129, 136
'margin of safety', 80
marginal rate, 28-9
market price, 121
maximax approach, 67-8
maximin approach, 67
minimax regret approach, 69-70

Modigliani-Miller approach, 59, 61-3
money
    time value of, 21-2, 26-8
    value (mortality rates), 121-2
Monte Carlo simulation, 21
Morgan, E.J., 116
mortality rates, 121-2
motorway scheme (CBA), 125
multi-period captial rationing, 40, 92-7
multiple IRRs, 41, 43
mutually exclusive projects, 36-8, 92

National Economic Development Council, 14
net current cost cash flow, 101, 102
net present value, 13, 14, 38-44, 135
    calculation of, 28-36
    expected values for, 82-3, 86-7
    IRR and (comparison), 42-4, 134
    linear programming, 93-4, 96-7
    merits (summary), 41-2
    public sector, 123
    single-period capital rationing, 89-92

operating costs, 107-9, 110-16
operating leases, 114
opportunity costs, 123
    of capital, 43, 47, 107
    minimax regret approach, 69-70
ordinary share capital, 54, 56

payback, 13, 14, 20-23, 25, 71-2, 133, 135
perfect capital market, 15-16, 33
    efficient market hypothesis, 17-17-19

Index

'pet' projects, 127, 130
Pike, 133, 134, 135, 136
political contributions, 104
polynomial equation, 33-4
post-audits, 128-31, 136-7
preference shares, 50, 51, 54, 58
prices
   adminstrative, 121
   market (in CBA), 121
   movements, 98-103
   shadow, 96, 121, 122
   share, 17-19, 47-50
probability, 13, 64-5
product life cycle, 74-5
profit, 11, 12-13, 22, 29
   accounting rate of return, 13, 23-5, 133-4
   after depreciation, 23-4
   retained, 14, 47-8, 56
   taxation of, 103-4
projects, 12-13
   authorisation, 128
   control, 128-30
   dependent, 40-41
   different initial outlays, 38-9
   independent, 33
   mutually exclusive, 36-8, 92
   'pet', 127, 130
   unequal lives, 39-40
public goods, 118-19
public sector, 117-26
purchasing power, 98, 100, 101

random walk pattern, 17-18
reinvestment assumptions, 40
replacement cost, 108-9, 110-11
replacement cycles, 107-14
replacement decisions, 106-7
   annual equivalent annuity, 110-14
   lease/buy, 114-16
   lowest common multiple method, 107-10
reservoir scheme (CBA), 126
residual values, 107-9, 110-11, 113-16
Retail Price Index, 101, 102
return on capital expenditure, 23
return on investment, 13, 23-5
risk, 11, 54, 64
   -adjusted discount rates, 71, 72-5
   -appraisal techniques, 135-6
   aversion, 68
   avoidance, 75
   capital asset pricing model, 50, 75-6
   decision tree analysis, 83-7
   expected values for NPV, 82-3
   gearing and, 45-6
   measures for dealing with, 71-5
   Monte Carlo simulation, 81
   payback, 13, 14, 20-23, 25, 71-2, 133
   sensitivity analysis, 13, 79-81, 130, 135-6
   systematic, 76-7
   unsystematic, 77-9

Sale, 14, 134-5, 136
scale effect, 41
scale of investments, 36-8
Scapens, 14, 134-5, 136
semi-strong form efficiency, 18, 19
sensitivity analysis, 13, 79-81, 130, 135-6
sensitivity ranking, 80
shadow prices, 96, 121, 122
share prices, 17-19, 47-50
'Simplex' method, 96
simulation
   Monte Carlo, 81
   sensitivity analysis, 13, 79-81
single-period capital rationing, 35-6, 89-92

Index

'slack' variables, 95
small businesses, 103
social costs/benefits, 117-26
soft rationing, 89
Stock Exchange, 17
stock relief, 104
strong form efficiency, 18-19
Sutcliffe, 11
synergy, 19
systematic risk, 76-7

taxation, 107
   allowances, 103, 104-6
      effect on debt capital, 53-4, 55-6
      effect on investment appraisal, 103-6
theory (and practice), 132-7
Tikkas, 14, 134-5, 136
time value of money, 21-2, 26-8
Tomkins, C.R., 116
traditional approaches
   payback, 13, 14, 20-23, 25, 71-2, 133
   return on investment, 13, 23-5
traditionalist approach (cost of capital), 59, 60-61

transaction costs, 15

U-shaped cost of capital curve, 60-61
uncertainty, 13-14, 64
   game theory method, 65-71
unequal lives, 39-40
United Kingdom, 132, 133, 135, 137
United States, 132, 135, 136
Unlisted Securities Market, 17
'unorthodox' cash flows, 33-4, 43
unsystematic risk, 77-9
urban renewal (CBA), 125

variance analysis, 129

weak form efficiency, 18, 19
weighted average cost of capital, 29, 54-5
   CAPM and, 75-6
   gearing and, 61-3
   use of (in appraisal), 56-9
'willingness to pay' approach, 122
'writing-down allowance', 105

yield method, 123-4